Help Over Handcuffs

Kim Del Valle Walker

PAGE PUBLISHING, INC.
New York, NY

First originally published by Page Publishing, Inc. 2018

ISBN 978-1-64214-871-8 (Paperback)
ISBN 978-1-64214-872-5 (Digital)

Printed in the United States of America

Introduction

So What!

Well, yeah, I was charged with an OWI (operating while intoxicated), but my last one was five years ago—so what!

My friends and family drink and use just as much as I do, if not more! No one's bugging them about their drinking or drug use!

Who are they to say anything about my use?
I'm an adult!
I work!
I pay my bills!
I never lost a job because of my using!
I used to be a heroin addict, now I just drink—so what!
Alcohol is legal!
I'm not sticking needles in my veins anymore.
I have legitimate pain, you know!
My doctor prescribed these meds!
I can quit any time I want to! I just don't want to!

These are examples of some typical responses people use when it may be suggested by someone that they may have an issue with mood-altering substances. The people that listen to these (often their loved ones) echo these sentiments because they want so desperately to believe they are true—that things are better or getting better. Their responses often sound like as follows:

He's not using heroin anymore. He just drinks occasionally.

She only drinks wine now, none of that heavy stuff.

Well, yeah, I called work for her and told them she was sick. I didn't want her to lose her job. She has kids to support, ya know!

I didn't call the cops because I don't want him to get in trouble.

Well, he promised me it wouldn't happen again, and it didn't for a long time. This was just a fluke. Besides, he was depressed about his friend overdosing.

She really does have pain, and the doctors cut her off from her meds. What else was she supposed to do?

If any of this sounds even somewhat familiar, I get it!

When my parents put me into treatment when I was sixteen, I wasn't ready to quit using substances! So what if I was high! I just wanted people to *stop* bugging me about my substance use until . . .

See the Judge—What?

"Eat up! Eat up! It's time to see the judge!" Like a railroad spike being driven into my brain while trapped in a foggy tunnel, I wondered, *Who the hell's annoying voice . . . Wait a minute . . . Where the hell am I?* I thought in a panic.

Like a comatose sloth, I tried to peel my listless body from the concrete floor. Dried blood and bruises speckled my arms and knuckles. As I looked around, I suddenly realized I must have blacked out and recounted other blackouts I came to from.

There was that Rush concert that I had missed, but that was because I took Quaaludes with Southern Comfort. Beer! If I drank beer with the Quaaludes and did some coke too, that was the ticket! I'd only have a patchy blackout. Oh, but that one blackout—I was only going to stop for a couple of beers after work. I can't believe I didn't come out of that blackout until after 10:00 PM. Thank God the emergency contact picked Gene up from day care! Maybe I was drugged!

My thoughts continued rambling as I took a bite of *something* that kind of resembled a sausage from the tray of food the jailer had placed through the door slot as I tried to recall if I took any drugs that I didn't remember taking. Confused, I tried to create a timeline in my mind: *Okay, this morning, wait, I guess it was yesterday. What day is it? I remember the look of contempt on my mom's face as she screamed at me about spending all my money on partying rather than saving money to get my own place. I remember that! Okay, I went out to get another job. Two restau-*

rants had hired me . . . Not only did I get another job, but now I had three. Of course, that still wouldn't be enough for my parents. Nothing was ever good enough for them . . . Oh, yeah, I dropped Gene off at the babysitter's . . . I wonder if they still have him. Shit! I stopped to have a drink on the way home . . . David! What happened with David? We were supposed to go out last night. Oh my god, wait a minute. Did she say judge? What the hell is going on?

"Let's go!" she ordered while she unlocked the cell door. "Turn around," she insisted.

Grabbing my arms, she twisted them behind my back, slapped my wrists into handcuffs, squeezed them tight, and yanked me down the corridor to an elevator.

"Where am I?"

"*Really?*" she snorted. "Why, you're in the Sarasota County Jail, missy," she replied in an overly southern twang dripping in sarcasm.

"What happened? What did I do? How did I end up in Sarasota from North Port?"

There was no answer from her. She just yanked harder on the handcuffs and pushed me in through the elevator doors. My heart raced, and panic flooded my body as I caught a reflection of myself in the shiny elevator walls. My face was either bruised, had mascara smeared all over it or both. My hair was a mess, and I was on my way to see a judge? *Oh my god, what the hell had I done?*

Walking into the courtroom, I recognized some of the people that used to come into our restaurant, the Silver Star. I had been their *regular waitress*, although I hadn't seen several of them in a year or so.

I had worked for my father in his restaurants from the time I was tall enough to wash beer mugs with one of those spinny-brushy thingies.

By the time I was a teenager, I hated it! *Well, except for waitressing. I liked having cash on a daily basis.*

6

Then, one busy afternoon, during the lunch rush, I had enough of my father's yelling and slamming things around, and in a restaurant full of customers, I told him so.

"You're a fucking asshole, and I quit!"

I grabbed my purse from under the counter. I looked at the customers that seemed to all be staring at me in shock and stated, "I'm sorry. I truly am sorry, but I *have to* leave."

And I left them all just sitting there, in various stages of their dining experience.

I walked out the door, jumped in my car, stopped at the corner store, bought a six-pack, and like so many times when I finished working, I went to my favorite sitting rock behind the Van Wezel Performing Arts Hall. I could chug beers, smoke a bowl, enjoy nature, the sound of the waves upon the rocks below, and wash away the rage and sadness that seemed to consume my soul.

Of course, when my father decided to close the restaurant, he blamed me. It seemed *everything was always my fault!*

As I walked past the people in the crowded courtroom, I tried not to make eye contact with anyone. I didn't want any of *my old regulars* to recognize me.

Oh shit! I almost blurted out loud. Two Sugars and a Splash of Cream (yes, I referred to many of my customers by what they ordered) suddenly appeared before us from behind the door. He looked the same except he was dressed in his black robe.

"All, rise," the bailiff boomed.

When my name was called, he just stared at me emotionless over his glasses. It seemed like minutes, and I looked down, unable to make direct eye contact with him. He read from some notes, which I presume, was the police report. He shook his head from side to side, as though he were disappointed, and then began to describe a drunk, violent, and out-of-control woman who was reportedly frothing at the mouth like a rabid dog and that spat, swore, and swung her fists at the arresting officers.

Then, the district attorney piped in. Pointing toward me with some papers he had in his hand, the anal, uptight-looking man stated, "Your Honor, this woman is a danger to herself and others. This is a woman who not *only* assaulted and battered *her own mother,* a woman currently lying in a hospital bed—"

Assaulted her mother? Hospital bed? Did I just hear that correctly?

"*What!*" I blurted out, unable to help myself. Judge Two Sugars and a Splash of Cream glared at me for blurting, and I immediately shut my mouth.

"This woman," the district attorney continued after also shooting me a glare, "also verbally attacked and screamed at her own father, and I quote, 'Look at me, you fucking child abuser, I'm a product of my environment!' End quote. Your Honor, the State moves to pursue—"

Shocked and horrified, I looked up and, unable to help myself, spontaneously blurted out, "Is my mom okay?"

"At this time, we're uncertain of your mother's condition," the judge replied.

A future court date was set, and I was surprised after hearing the State's desire to lock me up and throw away the key, that Judge Two Sugars and a Splash of Cream was actually letting me go. With a crack of the gavel, I was being yanked back to the elevator, to gather my belongings and be released on my own recognizance.

The problem: I was in northern Sarasota County, but I lived in southern Sarasota County. I didn't know where my son was *again,* and I beat up my mom? My stomach turned, and I wanted to just wake up from what seemed to be some horrible nightmare that I couldn't believe was actually happening.

"Which hospital is my mom in? Can I use the phone?" I rattled off to the officer.

"There's a pay phone down the street," he responded as he placed a brown paper envelope on the counter and handed me a paper to sign. Grabbing the three dollars and change, which I apparently came in with, I shoved it in my pocket and headed for the pay phone.

Sweating and shaking, I could barely get the quarter into the coin slot and dial the number to Venice Hospital. I gave my mother's name and was asked to hold on.

A nurse picked up and explained that my mother was refusing calls from me. She informed me that my mother had suffered a broken hip and jaw and had to have emergency surgery (this was before HIPAA or Health Insurance Portability and Accountability Act of 1996).

"She's shaken up and bruised up, but the surgery went fine. It'll probably be a good six to eight weeks for her to recover followed by weeks of physical therapy."

"Do you know where my son is?" I interjected, unable to listen to the reality of what I had done *to my own mother* any longer.

"No. I don't know anything about your son, but your father and brother were up here last night and this morning. Do you want to leave a message?"

"Yes, please. Please just tell my mom I am *truly* so *very sorry!*" I said horrified and with extreme-guilt-ridden sincerity.

My thoughts continued to race: *What the fuck was wrong with me? What kind of person beats up their own mother? And beats her up so bad that she breaks her hip* and *jaw?*

Feeling sick to my stomach, I hung up the phone and began pacing in circles, talking to myself, contemplating what to do next.

Maybe I could just thrust myself into the traffic? No! Someone else would get into trouble—shit!

What about Gene? I suck as a mom! I love him though. He loves me. I can't leave my little boy without his mom!

I beat up my own mother! What the fuck is wrong with me?

And that is when my "so what!" became my "now what?"

When My "So What" Became My "Now What?"

S haking, I inserted another quarter into the phone and dialed my ex-husband, Tracy, hoping he had our son, Gene.

Tracy was the lead guitar player of the band that had been booked to perform in one of the nightclubs at Telemark Ski Lodge in Cable, Wisconsin. I had given myself a much-deserved weekend off from running one of the family restaurants in Green Bay to go snow skiing and of course hit up the clubs and party a bit while I was there.

After his first set, Tracy and I struck up a flirtatious conversation, and by bar close, Tracy had invited me to the band's suite to continue the party. By daylight, it was obvious that a blizzard was in full swing. There were whiteout conditions, drifting mountains of blowing snow, and weather advisories for people to stay put. No one would be going anywhere until the storm let up.

Stranded on the other side of Wisconsin and closer to Minnesota than Green Bay, I called my father, who was in Florida at the time, to let him know that I probably wasn't going to make it back to the Green Bay restaurant by Monday morning, but that I'd try. As usual, he yelled at me and said if I weren't there on Monday, I was fired.

"Fine then, I quit!" I yelled back into the phone and then slammed it onto the receiver.

I felt really brave when I wasn't within range of him being able to grab me by my hair or arm and beat the shit out of me like he had so many times before.

Besides, I had always wanted to work at Telemark Ski Lodge since first going there as a child, so I went to their human resources department and was hired as a server. I knew it was going to be a blast working there, and I couldn't wait!

Once Tracy was aware of my new employment, he graciously invited me to stay at the band's home, which they rightly referred to as "Hungry Hollow," until I could find another place of my own. Of course, I never left.

That following spring, us Hungry Hollow inhabitants raced to the bank hoping that our checks wouldn't bounce, as so many others had due to the high vacancy rates, a hellacious, frigid winter, and poor management.

Making the *entire* payroll seemed to be an increasingly difficult task for Telemark, and without customers, my tips had dwindled as well. To make some cash, we packed up and did what any rebellious rockers would do: we went on tour.

While sex, drugs, and rock and roll consumed my life, my parents were attempting to reconcile their relationship after a three-year breakup via a geographical relocation attempt to sunny Sarasota, Florida, and they would send me weekly postcards and letters about how I should come to Florida and check it out.

Touring was great until the band manager disappeared with the money and left us stranded somewhere in Minnesota. Unsure what we should do, I invited Tracy to come and check out Florida with me.

We visited my parents in 1982, became residents, and got married in 1983. Gene was born in 1984, and by 1985, Tracy and I had split up and shared custody of our son.

"Hello."

"Trace, it's me. Did you hear what happened last night?"

"Apparently, *your boyfriend David* showed up, and he was so disgusted by your drunkenness, he decided to leave. Is that what you mean?"

I ignored the anger I heard in his voice. I needed to play it cool. I didn't want him to know I had lost our son in a blackout—again!

"I heard you wanted to chase after him. Your mom tried to take away your car keys, and you beat her up?" he questioned as though he was fishing to find out if I was in a blackout.

Avoiding his question, I responded with my own question (a manipulative tactic I had learned to use from my father to avoid answering a question), "Do you know where Gene is, and if he's okay?"

"Gene's fine. I guess he was at the neighbor's and was crying when he saw you get arrested and your mom get hauled away in an ambulance. I'm sure it was pretty traumatic for him, but he'll be fine. Your dad said that if you got out of jail and I helped you, he'd make sure that we lost custody of him. I'm supposed to get Gene from him tonight. Your dad also warned me that if he or your brother found you, they'd kill you. And I believe him, so you can't come here!"

"What an asshole! You've got to get Gene away from him, but in the meantime, are you going to help me?" I'm sure I sounded desperate because I sure felt desperate!

"I'll take you to First Step, and that's it!" he boldly stated. "At least you can stay there for a few days and then *maybe* after I have Gene back and things settle down a bit . . . well, we'll see."

"The fucking treatment center! Are you kidding? I don't belong in a fucking treatment center!" I yelled into the phone.

"Well, at least I can get our son back, you'll have food and shelter for a few days, and your dad *won't even think to look for you there.*"

"I'm at the corner of Ringling and Lime." I sighed, knowing my options were extremely limited.

"I'll be there in thirty minutes," he said and hung up the phone.

I Don't Belong Here!

66 **S**o, Kim, have you ever used cannabis to get high?" the lady asked.

"Well, yeah, but . . ."

"What about cocaine?"

"Well, yeah, but I quit smoking it back in October *on my own*," I replied, trying to prove to her that I didn't need to be in treatment.

"What about other amphetamines?" she continued, almost robot-like.

"Well, yeah, but—"

Cutting me off, she continued, "What about Quaaludes?"

"Yeah, but—"

"Valium? Xanax?"

"Well, yeah, but the Xanax was prescribed. I had a spastic colon from the stress of being my father's restaurant slave."

"Did you take it as prescribed?"

"Well, I did in the beginning, but then it wasn't working anymore, so I had to increase the dose," I responded, trying to legitimize my self-prescribed increase.

"What about LSD?"

"Yep."

"PCP?"

"Yeah."

"Other psychedelics?"

I was really getting frustrated with her questioning. It felt like she was asking me the same questions over and over.

"Of course I used those things!" I blasted. "If you had my family, if you were married to my ex, if you lived the life I did, you would want to be as fucked up as often as possible too! I never stuck a needle in my arm! I know AIDS is the big issue right now!" *At the very least, I wanted credit for that!*

"Sure, I blacked out a few times. Sure, I passed out a few times. It's not like I was in a ditch with a bottle of vodka in a brown paper bag or lying in some sleazy motel room bed with needles hanging out of my arms. I purified my cocaine with baking soda, not ether or other chemicals. I don't even use every day! I don't have a problem—really! I came here voluntarily. My dad's the alcoholic not me!" I ranted.

"Okay, Kim. Okay. I hear you! Just take a deep breath. Breathe with me, okay? I have only one more question to ask you. Are you listening?"

Of course, I was listening! She was the one who wasn't listening!

"Were you in control when your mom tried to take your car keys from you?"

Shocked, I could feel my jaw drop open in horror that she knew. How did she know? Suddenly, I felt tears beginning to well up in my eyes. I hadn't cried in years. I didn't want to cry. Crying made me weak, vulnerable, and powerless. I didn't want her, or anyone for that matter, to see my emotions. And before I knew it, emotion-filled tears uncontrollably bubbled to the surface. I tried to get a grip. I tried to get them to stop. I tried to hide them, but the tears poured out of me, and not just from my eyes, but from somewhere deep within me, a place that I thought had been buried and locked away a long time ago, and I couldn't stop!

Coming around the desk, the intake lady stood in front of me and placed her hands on my shoulders. "It's okay, Kim. It's okay to cry. Treatment is a safe place to feel all those feelings that you've numbed for so long."

The next thing I knew I had dropped my hands away from my face, wrapped my arms around her waist, and was blubbering into this woman's body.

"It's going to be okay. I'm really glad that you're here," she said so genuinely while she tried to comfort me.

Pulling back from her, I tried to compose myself the best I could. What did she mean she was glad that I was here? I certainly wasn't!

"Come on, let's get you settled," she said as she helped me out of the chair and led me through the halls to what would be my room for the next five to seven days. She introduced me to my roommate, brought me some toiletry items, a pair of scrubs, and some flip-flops, and laid them on my bed.

"Why don't you take a long hot shower and just get some rest for now? I'll come and get you when it's time for dinner. Then, tomorrow, you'll need to follow the schedule. It's in this folder right here," she said quietly as she placed it on the night-stand. "Do you have any questions before I leave you for now?"

"I'm really sorry for being so rude to you," I managed. "I'm really not that person," I mustered, sniffling back new tears.

"Most of us aren't," she replied. "We often lash out because we're frightened, hurt, and scared. Most of us have been through a lot before we get here—if we get here. It's going to be okay, Kim." She smiled reassuringly as she walked out and closed the door behind her.

I couldn't help but feel guilty for yelling at her. She was so patient and treated me so nicely. It seemed like she genuinely cared, even though I felt like I certainly didn't deserve to be cared about or treated nicely.

After taking a shower, I put on the scrubs that First Step had provided for me and climbed into bed. My roommate had disappeared, and I was grateful that I had the room to myself. I was still sore and exhausted, but my mind wouldn't rest. I couldn't stop thinking about how much I hated my father when he drank. It didn't matter to me that he had been sober since 1981. I hadn't forgiven him. I blamed him for the violence that I had inflicted upon my mother. Just like what I had apparently screamed at him—I was a product of my environment! I was the one that had tried to stop the violence in our family. I certainly never thought I'd be another perpetrator of it!

Northern Comfort

Finally getting the pillow just right, I closed my eyes, and out of nowhere, thoughts of my grandpa Wally, my father's father, popped into my head.

My grandpa Wally used to take me with him to all kinds of shows: boat shows, horse shows, dog shows, and live theater shows. He introduced me to people he referred to as "important or famous people," but the only one that I recognized was Michael Landon from *Bonanza*. (For you younger folks, Michael Landon also played the dad on *Little House on the Prairie*. He sadly passed away from pancreatic cancer in 1991.)

Before going to a show, my grandpa Wally would usually take me shopping. Teasing with a smile, he'd say the same thing each time, "You're going to need a new outfit if we're going to go to . . . [whatever show he was going take me to]." He'd have the salesladies help me and then have me come out and model for him. He would always ask me to twirl if I had a dress on. He knew that I loved frilly dresses that spun when I spun and would ask me if I thought it was a good one. Then, he'd always make sure that I had new shoes, a matching hat, gloves, or a new fur muff to match my new outfit. He made me feel so special when he'd take me out with him, but my favorite place to go with him was to his brother and sister-in-law's home.

My uncle Arnie and my aunt Elsie lived in this huge white house that, for a long time as a child, I imagined was similar to the one our president lived in. It was on the St. Charles River in

Illinois. They owned a marina that was just down the driveway from their home.

I had so much fun at their house. If I wasn't splashing around in the water, I'd be out in a boat or watching from the shore while my grandpa and uncle tested out new motorized inventions that they had created with my faithful companion Humphrey.

Humphrey was a huge cuddly Saint Bernard that seemed kind of mopey when he walked, but at the same time, he was always wagging his tail and seemed to have a perpetual smile on his face. Whenever Humphrey and I couldn't tag along with my grandpa and uncle, one of the staff would bring us up to the house.

Being in that house with all of its rooms, the other dogs (they had twenty of them), my aunt's pigeon that freely flew around and nested on top of one of the hutches was an adventure too. I just thought it was the coolest place ever, and I wanted to live there.

My favorite room in the house was my aunt Elsie's library. It was right there in the middle of a wall, but unless one knew there were doors there, one might never see it. It reminded me of a secret passageway, and it just added to my fascination of their home. To get into the *secret space*, one had to slide the big wooden doors into the side walls. Once inside the room with the doors closed, it felt even more magical. One whole wall was filled with books from the floor to the ceiling, and it even had a ladder that slid along tracks that my aunt used to push me on. Each time I entered the library, it seemed there was some new statue, knickknack, or ancient object that came from some archeological dig, from some faraway land that I hadn't noticed before. I was sure that the huge carpet in the middle of the room had certainly belonged to some magical genie from Persia that used to fly around on it until someone stole it and trapped him in a bottle. There was an assortment of interesting chairs with curvy wooden armrests that looked like lion and eagle claws with matching footstools. There were colorful lamps that had tassels and glass beads that sparkled and glowed when the light filtered through them.

This room smelled wonderful. It felt magical and safe. When my aunt Elsie would take me in there, she'd sit and read books aloud to me. I'd lie on that magic carpet, chin in my hands, knees bent, feet swinging back and forth with Humphrey right by my side. Sometimes I fell asleep on Humphrey, and he seemed more than happy to let me use him as a pillow.

Unlike being with my parents, my aunt actually encouraged me to ask questions about anything and everything. She even allowed me to interrupt her reading to ask questions right when I had them. I was allowed to eat on the floor from the fancy china, share with Humphrey, and my aunt would laugh at him when he'd slobber on me. If I ate all of my "good food first," I was always allowed to take a handful of the M&M's from the candy dish that she always had filled on her writing table. Humphrey liked the M&M's too. It was absolutely wonderful.

When I was older, I heard my aunt used to have séances in that room, and that she did what the family called "automatic writing", in which she would go into a trance, and pass along messages from departed loved ones on the other side. She had even given me some books on the subject of spiritualism and ESP, although I didn't read them until I was a teenager.

I always felt loved and safe at their house. *Maybe that's why I was thinking about them? I sure could use some protection and guidance from their spirits right now, along with Humphrey as my pillow.*

Unfortunately, after we moved from Illinois to Wisconsin, when I was ten years old, I never saw my grandpa again. And the last time I saw my uncle Arnie was at my aunt Elsie's funeral. When my mother and I were about to leave my aunt's casket, my uncle Arnie walked over to us. He looked into the casket one more time, turned toward us with tears in his eyes, reached inside his jacket pocket, and pulled out a royal-blue velvet jewelry box.

"Make sure Kim sees," he said as he handed it to my mom and took his hanky out to wipe his tears. Looking at me, my mom slowly opened the box so the both of us could see its contents at the same time. My mom gasped, and I was mesmerized by the brilliant white star that exploded from the blue stone that was surrounded by glistening diamonds. With tears still welled in his eyes, he put his arms around both of us and instructed my mother to make sure that the ring was given to me one day, when I was older.

When my parents weren't home, I'd sometimes sneak into my mom's lingerie drawer, take the ring box out of the sock that she had it hidden in, carefully and sneakily take it out of the box, and put it on. For some reason, when I'd put my aunt's ring on my finger, I felt magically transported to wonderful memories of times spent with her, Uncle Arnie, and Grandpa. It felt like they were all right there with me, still comforting me, still loving me. *I'll probably never be given that ring now,* I thought.

Why Do We Keep Doing This?

I was emotionally drained, but I still couldn't stop thinking about the times I'd spent with Grandpa Wally, Aunt Elsie, and Uncle Arnie. Whenever I came home from their house, I wanted to share my excitement with my parents, show my dad the new outfits my grandpa had bought for me, tell my dad about what great adventures we had—shows, shopping, stories about Humphrey and the other dogs, funny contraptions that my grandpa and uncle sank and the hilarity of them swimming back to the shore, or contraptions that they made that sounded like they might explode at any moment, as well as the excitement that everyone had when one of those contraptions actually worked. But I couldn't.

I quickly learned not to talk about any of it because it seemed to really piss my father off. My mom would listen nervously as though my father might overhear me. Then, she would hurry, put everything I brought home with me away, and remind me not to tell my father, so he wouldn't get angry.

Whenever anyone mentioned Grandpa Wally, my dad would always say, "That good-for-nothing drunk!" But I loved my grandpa, and I felt sad that I couldn't tell my father how wonderful I thought he was.

Then, one evening in 1976, I learned more. I answered the phone. My grandfather's wife, Alma, asked to speak to my father right away, so I knew it must be important.

Curious about what was going on, I took a seat at the kitchen table to eavesdrop. I heard my father yelling into the phone at her, and then he stomped back into the kitchen, slammed the phone down onto the wall, and headed straight for the liquor cabinet. He grabbed a new bottle off the shelf, plopped into the chair across from me at the kitchen table, cracked it open, and took a big swig.

My mom said nothing and sat down at the table too.

"He's dead. That son of a bitch is finally dead. And no! We are *not* going to the funeral!"

I wanted to cry, but was afraid to because I knew my father wanted me to hate him like he hated him.

It would be the night my grandpa Wally passed away that I first heard about cirrhosis of the liver and gained some insight into my father's hatred toward his father.

The more my father drank, the angrier his rants became and the more paralyzed with fear I became of what he might do to me if I showed any emotion or tried to get up and go to my room. So I sat there. I tried to be as expressionless as possible and swallowed each lump that formed in my throat to keep any sign of my sadness from being exposed.

My father told story after story of my grandfather's and great-grandfather's drunken rages, how they had both cheated on and left their wives and how they had beaten them and my father for years. My father spoke of multiple occasions where he had to clean up the blood from his mother's and grandmother's faces, jump into fights to get his father off his mother or his grandfather off his grandmother, and how he became the punching bag on their behalf. He called them "violent men," who would spend all the money on "booze, broads, and the ponies," men that would disappear for days, weeks, and even months at a time and how they never paid child support.

"I wanted to kill that son of a bitch," my father stammered, pounding his fist on the table. "My mother had to work two full-time jobs . . . I had to drop out of school in the eighth grade to work . . . just to help support and protect my brothers from going through what I went through . . ."

Then, finally, after several hours and almost drinking the entire bottle, he passed out. With his hand still on the bottle, his head on the table, and his body slumped in the chair.

After a few more moments, my mom finally motioned that it was safe for me to go upstairs to my room. I had hoped to get at least a few hours of sleep before I had to catch the school bus, but I sobbed and gasped into my pillow instead, hoping that my father wouldn't wake up, hear me, and then beat me in his drunken stupor.

My grandpa Wally's death was the first time I understood my father's rage toward his father. It was the first time I understood his desire for his father's love, but seemingly wanting to kill him at the same time. I felt the same way. I wanted my father's love too, but at times, I secretly wished he'd die. I even had several dreams where I stabbed him in the back with a chef's knife—and not just stab him once, but I'd go all *Psycho* on his ass. I always felt guilty about those dreams after I had them.

The night my grandpa died, there were moments that I actually felt sorry for my father, but it quickly turned back to rage. *He knew what it was like to grow up like that. Why then had he repeated the same things in his own marriage and family? Why didn't he change things?*

And now here I am, lying in a bed, in a treatment center, repeating the same drunken violence. I never wanted to be like him! I never wanted to hurt someone in a drunken rage. Not only am I repeating the patterns of my father, but I'm just like my grandfather and his father before him! What the fuck? Why do we repeat this shit? Why do we keep doing this? Maybe they didn't know how to do things differently . . . That's no excuse! But I don't know how to either . . . I feel so hopeless! I feel like such a worthless piece of shit!

My Poor Mom

I remember the first time I saw him attacking my mom. I was about four. I woke up to her screaming for him to stop, jumped up and ran into my closet with my blanket and my statue of the Virgin Mary. My mom had told me that if I were scared, to "pray to her," and she would protect me.

Squishing myself as small as I could into the corner of the closet, I began praying for the screaming and yelling to stop.

"*Shut your fucking mouth!*" he screamed while she cried and begged him to stop.

Then, the only sound I could hear was what sounded like my mom gasping and kicking the floor. Too afraid to move but too afraid not to, I snuck out of the closet, peeked down the hall, and saw my father sitting on top of my mom. He had her arms pinned at her sides with his knees, and it looked like he was choking her.

In a panic, I ran to the phone in their bedroom and called my grandparents, and they instructed me to quietly go back to the closet and stay there until I heard the police.

Moments later, I could hear my mom coughing and crying. I didn't hear my father anymore, and I was scared that he had seen me and that I would be next. I remember closing my eyes tight and gripping my blanket and statue as though my very life depended on it until I heard the knock at the door.

I could hear men's voices and peeked around the corner of my bedroom door toward the living room while trying to be as quiet and invisible as I could. I needed to make sure it was the police.

Peering around the corner, I strained to listen and could hear my father telling the officers that he and my mom had been wrestling. I could tell that my mom had been crying, but heard her tell the police that everything was fine.

I remember wanting to go hug my mom and to tell the police what *really happened,* but I didn't because I was too afraid of what my dad would do to me if he knew the police were there because I called my grandparents.

The police weren't there for very long, but after they left, I remember struggling to stay awake just in case he went after her again. I was afraid if I fell asleep, he would kill her.

It would be years later that I found out that had not been the first time he had hurt my mom, but I quickly learned that it wouldn't be the last time either.

There were times she wore sunglasses when he had given her black eyes or a broken nose. There were times I watched as she rubbed makeup and powder on bruises to try and hide them. There were times I knew she was crying, but she'd tell me she had been cutting onions, although I never saw or smelled any onions. There were more times I knew she had been crying, but she would tell me she had something in her eye or that she had a cold and her eyes were "just watering."

Jesus Christ! I know what I saw! How the hell am I ever supposed to trust what I see and sense when I've been told that's not what was "really going on"? It's fucking crazy making is what it is! I'm twenty-two years old for God's sake! It's been like what . . . eighteen years since the first time I can remember that he beat her up? How many times over the years had he hurt her and made her cry? He was the one I should have beaten up, not my poor mother! I can't believe that after everything I've watched her go through, that I've hurt her now too . . . Why did she stay with him? Why didn't she leave back then? And why on earth after being away from him for almost three years, did she decide to try one more time? It's all about the fucking money! The opportunity to relocate to Florida! Did I beat her up because I'm really pissed off at her? Why didn't she leave him when he began abusing me? It was about the fucking money! Maybe I'm pissed because she didn't protect me? I want to get the fuck out of here! I need a fucking drink!

I Am *Not* One of *You*!
Leave *Me* Alone!

After being in detox for a few days, about the only thing I found even remotely interesting was learning about the "dis-ease concept" that the counselors were trying to get us to understand. I certainly felt in a state of dis-ease, but what I really wanted them to teach me was how to fix my fucked-up family. They were the ones that *really needed to be here* learning about this stuff!

I was only going to be twenty-three the following month; I certainly wasn't ready to commit to never drinking or drugging again. And First Step's treatment team had yet to convince me that I was the one with the problem and that I was the one that needed to change. "You need to keep the focus on yourself" was their answer each time I'd bring up my family. I really wanted them to know that beating up my mom was just a fluky, one-time thing that happened. I wanted them to know I was *not* the one with the problem and just agree with me, but *nooooo*!

Then, they'd try to divert my attention by asking me if I had begun working on or finished their first-step packet yet.

"No," I'd answer with a big sigh and an eye roll. I didn't need this shit, but my parents sure did!

I did agree with most of the First Step's "unmanageability questions." Beating up my mom, waking up not knowing where my son was, in a jail cell, in stranger's beds, under a parked semitrailer, and some other experiences wasn't exactly managing my life.

I understood that intending to stop for a couple beers or a couple drinks and ending up drunk or in a blackout was pretty unmanageable too. I could admit to that, but I certainly was not powerless over anything and especially not drugs or alcohol!

I didn't drink every day. I never missed work because I was drunk, high, or hung over. I pretty much only drank on weekends and smoked a little pot here and there. Hell, I quit freebasing coke back in October. But I also had nowhere to go and was afraid that if I didn't do what I was supposed to do while I was in First Step, they'd kick me out.

I also knew once I finished up their first-step packet stuff, they'd just give me more step questions, which meant I'd eventually get to the step with that *God* word!

I wanted *nothing* to do with God! Where the hell was God, Jesus, or his mother for that matter, when I needed them? That's right—nowhere to be found!

Now these treatment people were telling us poor saps that we had to sit through their stupid-ass meetings as part of our treatment too? Where "people from the outside are coming to have a meeting tonight, and it's mandatory that you all attend" bullshit!

My dad had dragged me to a few meetings after he got sober in Wisconsin. He did seem to handle things better when he went to the meetings, but once he had my mom back, he slacked off and seemed to be the same asshole he had always been. The only difference was he was an asshole without the alcohol, and I still hated him!

Every time I would hear him say things like "I'm cured" or "I'm recovered," I'd vacillate between wanting to punch him or puke!

Don't get me wrong, after moving to Florida, and before purchasing the Silver Star, he'd hang out at this tree on Siesta Key Beach, which they referred to as "Roy's Palm" with a bunch of other recovering people. They all seemed very nice, but they were also a bunch of old rich retirees that had no idea what my dad was *really like*!

If being a person in recovery meant spending my days with a bunch of sober, rich old fuddy-duddies, I'd rather be drinking and smoking a bowl behind the Van Wezel. Thanks, but no thanks!

There were also these YANA (you are never alone) Club people, who used to come into the Silver Star. They would take up my station for hours, which in restaurant language means, "You are keeping me from getting new tippers in those seats. Drink your damn coffee and fucking leave already!" But noooo, they'd sit around drinking their coffee for fucking hours, laughing and pretending they were all happy and shit, and they were shitty tippers too—unless Frank was with them.

Frank seemed like a real mental case, but he was a good tipper, so when he was around, I'd wait. And while I waited, I'd usually pour myself a beer, sit in a booth—where I was sure those drunks and druggies could see me—raise my mug and toast them. Since I knew those poor drunks couldn't drink anymore, I was happy do it for them. Cheers!

They're Going to See Me Here—Shit!

S itting in the back corner, where I was hoping to go unnoticed and possibly take a nap once the meeting got started, I tried to hide as I saw a combination of Roy's Palm retirees and the Silver Star Shitty Tipper Brigade bounce through First Step's doors, pretending like they were all happy to be there—what a joke!

Then, I saw Pat. My father considered Pat and her husband to be his friends. She was a nice woman who frequently asked me to join them for an "official meeting" at Roy's Palm. She even came to my baby shower, and now she was walking right toward me— and all I could think was, *Oh shit! There's nowhere to hide!*

"Kim! I'm so happy that you made it!" she said, smiling all happy and shit while she hugged me.

Oh jeez, here comes another one, I thought as another old fuddy-duddy made his way toward me.

"Kim, I thought for sure you had died out there after not seeing you for so long. Where've y'all been? We'll, at least, y'all made it here," another one of the retirees commented as he smiled and hugged me too.

My brain was buzzing with thoughts. *Why are you talking to me? Stop bugging me! Leave me alone! What the hell is wrong with you people and your fucking hugging? You can go away now! I have no interest in joining your cult!* Outwardly, however, I smiled, nodded, and attempted to be gracious.

Then, I saw Frank, and all I could think was, *Please, please, please, don't let Frank see me!*

I just wasn't in the mood to deal with Frank and his happy-ass weirdness. I used to watch him through the front window of the Silver Star doing some weird shit that he called "calisthenics." Whatever it was that he was doing was not calisthenics, but something that made him look even more mental than I already suspected him to be.

He ordered weird combinations of food that he was always suggesting I try. He'd invite me to join them at their table or to their YANA Club, and he was *annoyingly happy.* He did pick up other people's tabs and would leave at least a 20 percent tip for their bill too, which was nice, but the problem was just when I thought Frank would finally be leaving, someone else would join him, and the bullshit laughter would start all over again, and I'd be stuck waiting longer for them to leave. There was just no way he or anyone for that matter could possibly be that fucking happy, and I certainly didn't want him to see me here!

Oh, shit! Here we go!

"Hey, look, it's Kim!" He pointed at me and alerted the people coming through the door with him. "She made it!" he exclaimed all loud and excited-like. Smiling, his entourage followed him over to me, and of course, like the rest of these hug-happy mental people, he leaned over and hugged me too.

Standing back upright, he told me all his cult members' names—*like I gave a shit*, and they all hugged me too while my thoughts were, *Oh my god! Will you people just get the fuck away from me! I don't want you to see me here! I am* not *one of* you! *Stop bugging me!*

Again, I of course responded politely with more smiles, nice to meet yous, and affirming nods. However, secretly, I wanted to get up and run out the nearest door. I also hoped they didn't know what I had done to my mother!

Then, it suddenly hit me . . . *Holy shit! I wonder if it was in the newspaper . . . Nah, they wouldn't even come near me if they knew.*

Then, a younger girl named Karen, who came to the restaurant frequently, spotted me. I always thought if she were still partying, we'd be great friends. She came over and gave me a hug too. Then, she told me to slide over and sat down next to me. *So much for that nap!* I thought.

"You're looking pretty rough there, girl. This disease has really taken a toll on you, huh?"

I nodded in agreement while thinking, *A toll on me?*

"I heard what happened to your mom."

"You did?" I almost shouted, sitting up and turning directly toward her to read her facial expressions. Surely, there would be some sort of disgust or repulsiveness toward me from her, but I didn't feel it, I didn't see it, nor did I sense it, which really surprised me.

"I'm really sorry that your mom had to be hurt in order for you to get here, but at least you're here and not dead. It's really sad that sometimes it takes such tragic things to happen to get us here . . . And unfortunately, some of us never make it here . . . I'm really happy that your mom's doing better and that you're both still alive."

My thoughts raced some more. *How'd she find out? Shit! Did Pat, Frank, and everyone else know too? Why the hell are they being nice to me anyway?*

"My mom's doing better? Did you see her?" I immediately asked.

"No, but there was an announcement before the noon meeting the day after it happened. People in the rooms have been checking on her every day since then and giving updates. Then, before the noon meeting begins at the club, Frank's been asking everyone, if we could all take a moment to pray for healing for you and your family."

"Really?" I found myself surprised not only by saying that out loud, but that people were actually praying for us and even for *me*? I was shocked. My normal response to a comment like that would have been to roll my eyes, but I found their prayerful gesture to be touching, and I caught myself mid–eye roll and refrained.

"I was so happy to hear that you were here. I remember watching you slug those beers down at the restaurant. And how many times I could see you were all coked up."

"How'd you know that?" I blurted simultaneously with my thoughts.

"Oh, sweetie, coke was my drug of choice. When I first got clean and sober and came into the restaurant, you were a huge trigger for me. One look at your eyes and I wanted to be high like you. The longer I stayed sober though, something happened, and when I'd see you, I'd think, *That poor girl, she's one of us, and she just doesn't even know it yet. I sure hope she makes it out of this alive.* And the way your dad yelled at you and your mom . . . I'm really grateful that Frank hung out in the restaurant longer than he probably wanted to, to make sure you and your mom were going to be okay before he'd leave."

What? Really! I thought, sitting up straighter and glancing over at Frank.

"I guess the day you quit and walked out, Frank went in there shortly after you had left and helped the other server get through the lunch rush. He bused tables, washed dishes, and apparently spoke with your father about a few things. He even brought your father to a few meetings at the club after that."

The look of shock on my face must have cued Karen that I had no idea when she responded, "Oops, maybe I shouldn't have told you about that. I guess I just figured you knew. Frank just does stuff like that. He's a good man with a huge heart.

"When I first came into the program and had no money or food, Frank would announce that if there was anyone at the meeting that was hungry and had no money, to meet him at the Silver Star after the meeting, and he'd get them something to eat—no strings attached other than to pay it forward someday. That's how I got to know him. He's helped so many of us over the years, feeding us when we were hungry, being there when we needed someone sober to talk with. I guess he was there for you and your family too, but you didn't know it, huh? He'd never tell anyone what he did or what he does. He's much too humble for that. He's just a wonderful human being. Have you heard his story?"

"No," I answered, feeling myself getting choked up.

"Oh, hey, the meeting's about to start. Remind me to give you my phone number after. We can go to some meetings together. There's some really good ones with people our age. You're going to love this way of life."

My thoughts suddenly shifted to Frank. *Oh my god! Frank did that? Holy shit!*

I looked across the room at Frank sitting there with that huge dorky smile on his face, and he did one of those finger waves to me.

And that's when it hit me: *That's why Frank sat at the table for so long and picked up people's tabs. They weren't shitty tippers! They had no money and were hungry, and Frank would make sure they ate. Frank was like a human version of Humphrey—big, cuddly, mopey, always smiling Saint Bernard that rescued people when they needed someone to rescue them.*

And then a tear suddenly rolled down my cheek.

He was sitting around so long to make sure my mother and I were going to be okay? To protect us from my father's rage?

Another tear rolled down my other cheek.

He bused tables, washed dishes, and *took my father to meetings at the YANA Club?*

The tears were now flowing to the point of dripping from my chin and onto my lap.

And I made fun of him and thought he was mental?

Karen patted my thigh as though she were telling me it was okay to just go ahead and cry, and I did. I didn't try to bury my face. I didn't try to swallow the huge lump that was in my throat. I just let these tears flow.

These were tears I had never experienced before. These were tears for a man that had gone above and beyond not only for me, but also for strangers and for my family.

These were tears of gratitude.

Let the Meeting Begin

B anging a gavel on the table like he was a judge or something, the chairperson began the meeting with a moment of
silence and a bunch of readings from their sacred text, which they
referred to as the "Big Book."

I was still deep in thought about the things that Karen had
shared with me about Frank. There was no way I was going to
sleep through this now. I actually wanted to pay attention. As
people shared about what it was like for them, how they got into
treatment, and how life was for them now, I found myself feeling
appalled one minute and amazed the next!

I would never tell a room full of people that my best friend
was dead because I was driving drunk and crashed the car that
killed them. Or how my friend OD'd and I was the one that got
them the dope that they overdosed and died from!

I know what I did was messed up too, but some of these
people's family and friends had died as a result of their using. One
guy even talked about how grateful he was for landing in prison
and claimed it's what had saved his life.

The more I heard, the more I wondered, *How could these
people live with themselves after things that they had done? How
could they be smiling? Thank God, my mom didn't die as a result
of my blackout! Thank God I hadn't killed anyone—but there were
those times I wasn't sure myself, until checking my car for dents or
blood the next day after some heavy partying.*

After people talked about the horrible things that happened
to get them into recovery, they spoke of how this way of life had

now given them hope, meaning, purpose, and how they've had miraculous, life-changing things happen since. Dreams fulfilled, repaired relationships, wonderful new friends, a sense of purpose in their lives, jobs, and families. How living this way of life, they had gone from homelessness, helplessness, and despair to living lives beyond their wildest dreams filled with love, hope, and gratitude.

And all from going to these meetings? I wondered. *Working the same steps these counselors here wanted me to do? Getting a sponsor? What?*

I was just shocked when I looked at some of the people that talked about their lives. I would have *never* suspected that some of them came from where they came from or to have spent years in prison or to be alcoholics or drug addicts! I found it all very confusing.

As the chairperson was wrapping up the meeting, he held up a white poker chip and announced, "If there's anyone here tonight that would like to try this way of life, one day at a time, we offer you a white poker chip. After ninety days of continuous sobriety, we offer you a blue poker chip, and after a year or multiples thereof, we offer you a red poker chip. Is there anyone here tonight that would like a white poker chip?"

I don't know if it was the Roy's Palm retirees, the coffee-clutching restaurant crew, or that I was just sick and tired of being sick and tired of people bugging me about my drinking and drug use, but I wanted to feel happy like the people that spoke, and yes, as difficult as it was to admit, I wanted to be like Frank.

And the next thing I knew, I was out of my chair and walking toward the man holding the white poker chip. People were clapping. Frank and Karen were cheering, and when I went to take that white chip, the man grabbed me, hugged me, and before he placed the chip in my hand, he turned me toward the group and announced that tonight, I was the most important person in the room, as a newcomer to this way of life.

All I knew was that I certainly didn't feel like the most important person in the room! I felt like a worthless piece of shit for what I had done to my mother, for my previous thoughts and feelings about Frank, for being so fucked up that I had lost my little boy—again! I felt undeserving of such an outpouring of love. I wasn't ready to stop drinking. I wasn't ready to stop drugging. All I knew was that I just didn't want to hurt anyone anymore! I just wanted to possibly feel a little bit of that hope and happiness that all these other people seemed to feel.

When I got back over to Karen, she squeezed me tight and whispered in my ear how proud she was of me, and all I could think was, *Really? Even after knowing what I did to my own mom?*

Next on the agenda was forming a huge circle and holding hands with everyone. I didn't know what to do with that poker chip and was going to place it on the bench when Karen said, "No, Kim. Place it between our hands so the energy, prayers, and love from the group will be absorbed into it. That way you can carry all that love and energy with you wherever you go."

The crowd began as I hurried and placed it between our hands, "Our father who art in heaven . . ."

While I mouthed the words along with everyone, I was thinking, *Absorbing love and energy? Wait! Wasn't AA supposed to be some kind of a religious cult? What Karen said seemed pretty Aunt Elsie-ish to me, almost antireligious—but we were saying the Lord's Prayer. I'm so confused!*

After we finished the prayer, the Roy's Palm retirees, Frank's followers, and other members of "the program" as they called it, flocked around me, hugged me, and congratulated me. They said things like, "Welcome, Kim!" "Remember, kid, take it a day at a time." "Easy does it, but do it!" "Keep coming back."

And I thought, *Keep coming back? To what? Treatment?*

One person handed me this brochure of meetings in the area that they called a Where and When. Other people gave me their phone numbers. Others offered to give me rides to meetings if I needed one. One guy that some programmers referred to as "Old-Timer Rodeo Bill" told me, "If you feel like picking up a drink or a drug, kid, put that poker chip in your mouth, and when it melts, you can use, but while you're waiting, get your ass to a meeting!"

Linda

I met with my counselor the next day. She had heard that I had picked up a white chip the night before. She told me she was proud of me and gave me a hug.

"I don't think I've ever been hugged this much in my life!" I said, feeling unworthy.

"Well, I guess you're way overdue then," she said with kind smiling eyes. "Have a seat, and let's chat," she said as she motioned for me to pick a spot, grabbed a yellow legal pad and a pen, and sat down in an antique-looking chair.

I sat into the corner of the couch, grabbed the pillow next to me, pulled it into my body, wrapped my arms around it, and looked around.

Although Linda's office felt comfortable, I was nervous. There were shelves adorned with books and archeological-dig-looking knickknacks. There were colorful abstracts, with inspirational sayings that hung on the walls and plants that made it obvious that Linda had a green thumb. It was like a modern-day version of my aunt Elsie's library, which I found comforting. There was even a dish of M&M's on her desk like my aunt used to keep. When she saw me look at the candy dish, she smiled and said, "Go ahead. Help yourself. Those are my mini miracles, and I'd be happy to share some of mine with you."

"What?" I asked confused as I stood up and took a few from the bowl with the little silver serving spoon that rested on the rim of the crystal dish.

"The M&M's, I call them my mini miracles," she replied, still smiling.

"Oh, M&M's, mini miracles . . . I get it!" I said, looking at the *m* that was stamped on each piece of the colored candies and then put an orange one in my mouth.

"You'll often hear people in recovery say, 'Stay around long enough until the miracle happens.' New people often feel hopeless and helpless, so until they experience or recognize how miracles are truly happening in their lives, even the often seemingly unpleasant ones that get them here, I offer them some of my mini miracles. And like M&M's, the sweetness in people's lives is usually just below the crunchy outer shell. Any way . . . help yourself." She paused and then continued, "As long as my bowl is full, you are always welcome to have some. And if my bowl is empty and yours happens to be full, *then* you have enough to share with others. It's important for me to always keep my bowl full."

"Was that just a metaphor for something I'm supposed to learn from you using M&M's?" I said and smiled while enjoying the chocolate.

Smiling, she answered, "Very good, Kim. I hope that one day you will have a full bowl of M&M's too, but until then, look for others who have enough to share with you. So tell me about yourself," she stated, leaning toward me.

"What do you want to know? My M&M's are melting in my hand and not in my mouth?" I chuckled as I thought of the M&M's slogan. *"M&M's, they melt in your mouth and not in your hands."*

Chuckling back, she said, "Our lives can happen like that sometimes, when we try to hang on to things for too long. Sometimes, we end up with a mess on our hands rather than letting go and enjoying the sweet miracle that's within our grasp. Well, how about if we start with how old you were when you first drank alcohol?"

"Hmmm, I don't really remember ever not drinking alcohol."

"What do you mean?" she questioned.

"It was just always around. I remember getting my dad cans of Schlitz and pronouncing it 'shits' and my dad and his friends laughing. If I went and got him a beer, he'd always let me have a drink of it."

"How old would you say you were?"

"I don't know, maybe four?"

"So do you remember the first time you got drunk?"

"I remember we were in Oshkosh, Wisconsin, at some parade."

"Who is 'we'?"

"My parents and I, it was cold, and it started raining, so we went into a bar, and they gave me a shot of Blackberry brandy to sip on—to warm me up."

"And you got drunk?"

"No. But I remember them getting me another one and feeling tipsy when I went to get off the bar stool."

"Do you recall how you felt about being 'tipsy'?"

"I remember them laughing at me and me liking how I felt, but that's about it."

"Do you remember how old you were then?"

"I want to say maybe six—maybe eight? Although my brother would have been around, but I don't remember him being there."

"So did your parents let you drink with them often?"

"Oh, yeah, in Wisconsin, as long as you're with your parent or parents, kids can sit in the bar, even at the bar and drink alcohol too—if their parents let them."

"So tell me about your first experience with drugs."

"I grew up in a neighborhood full of boys and hung out with them. I preferred dirt bikes to dolls, sports to playing house, and hanging with the boys over those prissy, catty girls any day. There was only one girl in the neighborhood anyway, and I think she played with dolls until she was like fourteen," I responded with an eye roll.

"The guys were like brothers to me. Well, until I started developing breasts. That's when things began to change. A few of the boys teased me about 'stuffing' and would try to get me to show them my boobs to prove that I didn't."

"And did you?"

"Oh, hell no! Sorry about that. I tend to cuss sometimes."

"No problem. It's not like I haven't heard it before, and I'm sure now that you've decided to try to clean up your act, you'll try to clean up your mouth too?" she questioned.

"Oh, yeah," I replied nodding, but thinking, *What? Just because I've decided to try and stay clean and sober, I have to quit swearing now too?*

"So what did you do when these boys wanted to have you show them your boobs?"

"I'd usually punch them and call them pigs. Then, they'd laugh and we'd go back to whatever fun we were having."

"Okay, back to your first drug use," she said, looking at her paper and getting ready to jot more notes down. "Tell me about that."

"One day, the neighbor boy, Randy, shouted out his bedroom window to me when I walked out of the door. He told me to come up to his room. He said he wanted to show me something . . ." I paused, almost as though I were time traveling back to that day, that moment.

"And?" Linda prompted me to continue.

"Randy was my friend Jerry's older brother. After summer vacation, he would be going into high school. I would be going into middle school, and I just happened to notice that he'd actually gotten kind of cute over the summer. I had been in their house a bunch of times over the years. Our parents were best friends. So I went in through the side door and ran upstairs to his room."

"Where were his parents?"

"Oh, probably working. His parents owned businesses too like my parents did, so they were always working."

"Okay, so you went up to his room and . . ."

"And his room was dark, but inviting. One of my favorite Led Zeppelin songs was spinning on the turntable. The sound, the rhythm, vocals, and the guitar were symphonically culminating in the middle of his room from the four huge speakers located in each of corners of his room. There were glowing purples, oranges, reds, and greens bursting from the black-light posters that hung on the walls, and the smell of strawberry incense swirled around in the purple light as though it were dancing to the music . . . It was hypnotic . . . magical, and I hadn't even smoked any pot yet," I giggled.

"I can tell by the way you're looking as you're describing this, that this was probably a very pleasurable experience for you," she interjected.

"Well, it began that way anyway."

"So what happened?"

"Randy was sitting on his bed leaning against the wall, like it was a couch. He told me to close the door and patted the bed next to him—to sit next to him. That's when he pulled out a bag of pot and proceeded to roll a joint in a purple paper. Putting it up to his lips, he lit it, and then he put it up to my lips. He told me to 'just suck in slowly and hold it,' and I did," I said, looking back at Linda wondering what she wanted to know next.

"That's it, Kim? Come on. I know you've got more in there," Linda prompted again.

Taking a deep breath, I let out a sigh and continued, "Well, when he held it to my lips the first time, I coughed. When he held it up to my lips the second time, I coughed again. The third time, he told me to turn my head toward him and open my mouth a little bit. Then he put the joint backward into his mouth, looked directly into my eyes, and blew the smoke slowly, and rather sensually, from his mouth into mine. That time, I didn't cough at all."

"If you had to describe your overall feelings from that experience, how would you say you felt?"

"I felt . . . I don't know . . . I just know that I really liked it! Not just the pot, but all of it—the black-light posters, the music, the smell of the pot mixed with the scent of the strawberry incense, and the excitement of it all . . . I think I felt . . . um . . ." Trying to figure out my overall feelings, I glanced upward to take myself back to that day. "Free . . . yeah, I felt free."

"Okay, so when I first said to you that this sounded like a pleasurable experience, you said that it began that way, what did you mean by that?" Linda asked.

"Well, after the joint was about halfway smoked, he put it out in an ashtray, leaned back toward me, and kissed me. It was also my first *real* kiss."

"So what else do you remember?"

"I liked kissing like that—a lot! As we continued kissing, I slowly ended up lying on his bed with him on top of me. Then, he put his hand up my shirt. As his hand got closer to my boob, I panicked. I pushed him off me, jumped off his bed, said 'I gotta go!' and I ran out of his room, down the stairs, and out the door kind of wondering what the heck just happened."

"So you didn't go back there? Did you tell anyone? Like your mom? What happened?"

"Hell, no, I didn't tell my mom! Oops, sorry about that," I apologized, aware that I had sworn again.

"It's okay. At least you're becoming aware of your cussing." She smiled. "So what happened then?"

"I went back again the next day."

"You did," she stated while not seeming surprised. "Thinking back on that day now, what do you think prompted you to go back?"

Pausing for a moment, I finally spoke, "Looking back at it now, I don't think it was because I wanted to get high. I think it was because I just wanted to experience those feelings again. I wanted to be kissed like that again. I wanted to be held like that again. I wanted to feel free and loved all at the same time.

"When we'd get high, we'd make out and talk for hours. Randy actually listened, and he seemed to really care about me. He even told me that he loved me a couple of times. And I told him things that I hadn't told anyone before."

"Like?" Linda asked.

"Like how I was adopted, felt unwanted, and how I had over-heard my mother talking on the phone one day and telling the person that they had adopted me to save their marriage. How my mom seemed to love my brother more. How there were times I wanted to run away and find my real parents."

"So wait a minute, your real parents?"

"Yeah, I'm an adoptee."

"Wait a minute, Kim. You're an adoptee?"

"Yes, ma'am."

"And your brother was adopted too?"

"Yes, ma'am."

"Okay, unfortunately, I'm sure there's a lot to explore as far as being an adoptee goes, but due to time, we're going to have to set that to the side for now and come back to it another time. So could you tell me a little more about when you said you 'just wanted to experience those feelings again'?"

"Well, eventually I was sneaking booze out of my parent's house to share with Randy, and we drank and smoked pot together. I felt free to be me when I was with Randy."

"What do you think kept you from being free when you weren't with Randy?"

"My parents, but you certainly don't want to open that can of worms right now. We'll be here all day," I kind of chuckled.

"Okay. That's another thing I really hope that we can explore together, but we really have to wrap things up soon, so before we finish this situation with Randy and getting high the first time, let me see if I can summarize what you've told me so far. So you and your brother are adopted. You felt unloved and unwanted—like your parents adopted you not because they wanted you, but to save their marriage. Alcohol has always been a part of your life ever since you can remember. You were about twelve years old when the neighbor boy, Randy, first got you high. He provided you with a space and place to feel loved and experience freedom, but those feelings involved smoking pot, drinking alcohol, visual and sensual stimulation. You ended up at First Step after being released on your own recognizance from jail due to being arrested—in a blackout for assault and battery, in which you beat up your mother. You were charged with drunk and disorderly conduct, assault, and battery. You have a two-year-old son who is currently safe with your ex-husband. You're currently jobless and homeless, and you picked up a white chip last night at the meeting . . . Do I have this all correct?"

"Yeah, you do!" I responded shocked that she got it all and pleasantly surprised that someone had actually listened to me.

"So you and Randy were drinking, getting high together, and making out. Let's take it from there."

"When I told him how I hated living in my house, he'd kiss me and wrap his arms around me. He made me feel like everything was okay even if it was only for a little while."

"So wait a minute. Did he force you to have sex with him? Did he rape you?"

"No, no, no. He didn't rape me. And no, I didn't have sexual intercourse with him, but he wanted me to. I feel kind of embarrassed talking about this stuff."

"I know. The reason I'm asking is because I really want to help you. In order for me to do that, the better picture I have of your life, the better idea I'll have to know how to best help you. Your secrets are safe with me, Kim."

For some weird reason, I felt like I could trust Linda, and I didn't trust many people anymore, but I felt safe in her presence and continued.

"Well, after continually refusing to have intercourse with him, one day he just pushed my head down there and told me to just put it in my mouth, and I did. I had no clue what the hell was going to happen. I was choking. I wanted to stop, but he was holding and moving my head. After he came or maybe I should say 'ejaculated,' I was so grossed out and scared, that I jumped up and ran home like I had the first time he tried to touch my boobs.

"I flung open the door to our house, ran upstairs, brushed my teeth, gargled, and then went into my bedroom and flopped onto my bed. I was really scared that my mom would somehow find out and tell my dad. If my father found out, he'd kill us both! You know, Linda, you're the first person I've ever told this to."

"Thank you for trusting me enough to do so. I want you to feel safe with me, like you can tell me anything. I truly want to help you live the life that you deserve, Kim, and to help you so that you don't have to wake up out of a blackout in a jail cell ever again. So did you end up losing your virginity to Randy?"

44

"No. After giving him a blow job that day—sorry, I guess I could have said, after performing fellatio or something less crass. I quit going over there. The first day of school was only a few days away, and we weren't going to have the free time, like we had over the summer anyway, so I tried to just put it all out of my mind. But when I went to the bus stop that first day of seventh grade, the guys of the neighborhood didn't greet me like they usually did other than a nod and hello. And then I saw it . . . written in huge chalk letters upon the pavement 'Kim is a whore.' I was devastated and knew that Randy had to have been the one who had written it. In that moment I saw the bus coming up the road, I turned around and ran back to my house instead."

"Was anyone home?"

"Yeah, my mom was, and she was pissed that I was missing the bus."

"Did you tell her what happened?"

"Well, I told her about the writing on the street."

"What did she do?"

"She angrily started getting dressed to give me a ride to school and asked me what I did to have someone write that about me."

"So your mom wanted to know what you had done to justify someone writing on the road that her daughter was a whore?"

"I guess so, but I was used to her doing that."

"Doing what?"

"Always making everything my fault," I responded.

"So let me clarify here, the one person you had trusted over the summer rejected you when you wouldn't have sex with him, forced you to 'give him a blow job.' You felt rejected by your friends at the bus stop, and then your mom didn't comfort you or talk with you, but was angry because she was going to have to give you a ride to school and wanted to know *what you did* to justify you being called a 'whore'?"

"Jeez, Linda, it sounds pretty bad when you put it that way."

"Oh, Kim, it's not bad, but it is terribly sad! That's a lot for a young woman just going into seventh grade to deal with! Did you cry?"

"Hell, no, I didn't cry."

"Did you just catch how you sounded proud about not crying?"

I did, but I didn't really know why, so I shrugged my shoulders instead.

"You also said that you never told anyone about this before, until today. Wow, Kim, it sounds like you've had to deal with some pretty heavy feelings on your own for a long time. Ouch," Linda said, putting her hand on her heart.

"Oh, there's no ouch there. Randy's family ended up moving away several months later anyway. I'd see him once in a while, but I never really talked to him again."

"So how did you deal with the pain of Randy's rejection and never talking to him again?"

"I just moved on," I responded, shrugging my shoulders again.

"Speaking of moving on, your discharge date is Monday, the ninth. What are your plans when you leave here?"

"Can I stay here and go through the twenty-eight-day treatment program?" I had no idea where that came from. It just came bursting out of my mouth.

Sitting up straight with a big smile on her face, Linda said, "You know what, Kim? I think that sounds like a great idea! I will have to check into some things, but I can let you know by the end of the day Monday. Either way, we'll have a plan for you. We're not going to just kick you out into the streets. How's that sound?" she said. Standing up, she set her legal pad and pen on her chair, opened her arms, and gave me another hug. "Here, before you leave, take some more miracles with you—take a handful, watch for them and expect them. If you stay clean and sober long enough and follow the suggestions, concepts, and ideas that you're learning, you'll be well on your way, Kim, to a new life that will seem miraculous. I promise." She smiled, reaching for her M&M dish to offer me some more.

"Thank you, Linda," I said as I took a handful of M&M's. "Oh, not just for the M&M's, but for . . ."

"I know, sweetie. Thank you for being so open and honest with me—for trusting me. I'm really glad you're here. I'll come find you before the end of the day Monday, as soon as I know if we can get you into our twenty-eight-day program," she said, walking out into the hall with me.

"Thank you, Linda. I truly appreciate it." And I truly meant it.

I Can't Believe I'm Doing This

I don't know what happened to me after meeting with Linda that Friday. Maybe it was because she gave me hope, hope that even *someone like me*, who felt as worthless and undeserving as me, could actually experience M&M's and have a happy life, regardless of the circumstances that got me here.

Maybe it was because it felt so good to tell someone, who was willing to listen to me without feeling like she was judging me. Maybe it was the feeling of genuine concern and care that I felt from her. I wasn't sure why I had suddenly decided that I wanted to stay for the twenty-eight-day program either, but I was beginning to feel better than I had in years, and I wanted that to continue.

I carried my white poker chip around in my bra hoping to absorb all that love and energy into my heart that Karen spoke of. It also reminded me that although I still wasn't ready to commit to never drinking or doing drugs again, I could try not to one day at a time, just for today. I knew that if I looked at it like a *forever thing*, or if I had somewhere else that I could have safely gone, I would have said, "Screw this!" and ran out the door.

Then, something seemed to shift in my thinking, and I thought, *Hmm . . . maybe instead of feeling trapped with nowhere else to go, maybe I could learn to handle drinking occasionally or doing a line here or there? If I just worked through this stuff from my childhood . . . maybe I could have the best of both worlds?*

According to Frank, Karen, Pat, and others, their happiness stuff seemed to only come from their recovery stuff, which

48

*involved no drinking or drugging though . . . Maybe I could just
use "socially"? I just don't want to hurt anyone again. I just want
to be happy. I just want to be a good mom. I want Gene to grow
up not just knowing he was loved, but feeling loved by my actions,
not just my words or financial payoffs. I want Gene to have a different life than I had. I want him to be happy. I want to put an end
to and learn how to stop the intergenerational drunken abuse and
insanity that seems to have gone on forever!*

And then it dawned on me. I had sworn I would never do
what my dad did, and he had sworn not to do what his dad had
done, and yet for multiple generations, we had continued this
same pattern, and then I thought, *I have to figure this stuff out!
If I don't learn how to do something different from my father,
grandfather, and his father before him, I'm destined to repeat the
insanity myself and pass it along to my son.* And that scared the
crap out of me!

I practically bounced down the hall and back to my room,
but when I got to the door, I suddenly stopped. I looked down
into my hand and counted how many M&M's I had left: eight. I
only had eight left, and suddenly it hit me. How many times had
I looked into my hand and counted how many pills I had left?
How many times did I count them to try to figure out how many
I was going to need and how many I could sell? How many times
had I stood there watching the cocaine that I *was* going to sell
disappear, get cooked up and smoked by me instead? How many
times did I say to myself, *Just one more* or *just one more time? I
just need this one more line, this one more hit, just one drink to
take the edge off?* How many times did I have a handful of God
only knows what, with no idea if it would kill me and take them
anyway just to feel different? What was it that made me do these
things regardless of how badly I wanted to do things differently?

Standing there looking at those M&M's, I realized that I
wanted the same thing from them—to just feel different. I wanted
the promise that they seemed to hold. Did I want to experience
eight mini miracles, one at a time? Or should I eat them all at
once and try for one big miracle?

As I stared into my hand, I suddenly thought, *Oh my god, am I thinking like an addict? No, these are M&M's, Kim!*

I reassured myself and decided to share my M&M's with my roommate and thought, *Four for her and four for me. Four mini miracles for each of us. That's what Frank would do.*

I slowly opened the door, and the room was empty. My roommate was gone, and I started laughing and talking to myself out loud. Well, there you go ding-dong! Instead of just going into your room, offering some to your roommate, you stood outside the door treating your M&M's like they were your stash, not wanting to share, and now all you have is a mess in your hand!

I continued laughing out loud—all by myself. I hadn't laughed in a while either, and it felt pretty darn good, and I remember thinking, *Ha, if someone saw me laughing all by myself right now, they'd think I was mental . . . Like Frank . . . Hahaha!*

Still laughing out loud, I threw all eight of the M&M's into my mouth, all at once, and went into the restroom to wash the mess that had been created from *"holding onto them for too long,"* I thought, making myself laugh out loud even longer off my hands.

When I came out of the restroom, I realized I had no idea where I was supposed to be. I hadn't seen anyone else when I was standing in the hall—*thank goodness!* They would have thought I was crazy, standing in the hall, staring at my hand, talking, and laughing out loud all by myself.

Still giggling at what a mental case I would have looked like to anyone that saw me, I picked up the schedule in my folder to see where I was supposed to be: "Free time." *Hmm, free time?*

Then, suddenly out of nowhere, something from somewhere inside my head said, "Pray!"

Looking around the empty room, I thought, *Where the hell did that come from? Oh, shit! I'm hearing voices now?*

I had more faith in the M&M's than I did in prayer! After all those times I had prayed for my father to stop drinking—*wait a minute, I guess he did stop drinking eventually, but what about all those other times?* There were so many times I put this "God" to the test only to continually be disappointed. My prayers always seemed to fall on deaf ears and after what I did to end up here—*pfff!*

My thoughts about this "God idea" continued, *Even if there were a God of some kind, "it" certainly had no time for me!*

And the next thing I knew, I was literally down on my knees. My hands were clasped and rested on my bed. My head was bowed, and with all the sincerity I could muster, I prayed to a God that I really didn't believe in.

Hello? If you're there, I know I haven't believed in you. I know I've done some really shitty things—oops, sorry about that! But if there is any way you could please help me out . . . I don't want to make you any promises that I might not be able to keep, but if you could arrange it so that I could stay in treatment . . . well . . . it would just really mean a lot to me!

Please don't be offended that I'm doing this, if you are really there, but I'm also going to ask some of my deceased loved ones for some extra help and support too—just in case okay? Okay . . .

Grandpa Wally, Aunt Elsie, Uncle Arnie, Humphrey . . . Anyone up there, out there, or wherever you may be . . . If you can hear my thoughts, it would really mean a lot to me . . . I think—to go through this treatment program here. If there's any way some of you can work some magic, pull some strings, align the sun, the moon, and the stars to make that happen—well, again, no promises, but I sure would appreciate it! Thank you! Amen. Oh . . . PS. I miss you all and love you all very much too!

Growing up Catholic, I didn't know how else to end this prayer, so I did the sign of the cross and chanted the words, "In the name of the Father, the Son, and the Holy Ghost. Amen."

Waitin' on Monday

Monday couldn't come fast enough. I tried to occupy my time playing chess, checkers, badminton, volleyball, reading stories in the back of the Big Book and discovered that I loved the one by Dr. Paul O, "Doctor, Alcoholic, Addict." I liked that story so much that I actually found myself laughing out loud and asked others if they had read it. Sunday night, after a meeting and before lights out, several of us read it out loud together. It had been the first time some of the other detoxies had read any of the book, and we concluded that maybe that book wasn't so bad after all.

With my roommate gone, I didn't have anyone to talk with before falling asleep or during free time. As tired as I was, when I'd try to fall asleep, my mind would go into overdrive with memories of my childhood crap, my mother, son, my probably now ex-boyfriend, David, and what the future might hold for me. It seemed the only way I was able to put my thoughts to rest was to write until my mind was empty enough to finally sleep.

I had always loved to write, so I was grateful for the time to do so. It was the one place that I could get my thoughts and feelings out. At one point, I even wanted to pursue a career as a writer or photojournalist. My high school English teachers encouraged me to consider going to college for journalism, but that was just not going to happen.

Whether I was performing in plays, playing in bands, singing in choirs, writing, or taking pictures, my father scoffed at the things I loved and was most passionate about.

"You can't make a living doing that!" he'd say whenever I had the guts to tell him what I wanted to go to college for, and I found myself feeling even worse about myself for even entertaining such thoughts. Then, I'd flip my thoughts to blaming him, *He has no idea who I am. He has no idea what I love, enjoy doing, or how I believe that with the right college education, maybe I could make a living doing "that"! But no!* His responses were always about making as much money as one possibly could. I just wanted to be happy, and growing up with money certainly didn't seem to be making anyone in our house very happy!

It was nice living in a big house, having nice clothes, going to fancy parties and fine restaurants. I liked having snowmobiles, dirt bikes, boats, horses, and stuff, but what I really wanted was to feel like I mattered—like my thoughts, feelings, emotions, accomplishments mattered. I wanted the kind of parents that would come to my school performances. I wanted to be able to look out into the audience and see them smiling and clapping. I wanted them to be proud of me. I wanted them to come to my sporting events and cheer for me, like the other parents did for their kids. Instead, everything involved alcohol, and once the drinking began, it was only a matter of time before all hell would break loose. That's when money and the things that money could buy became more like payoffs for me than something to enjoy.

"Why didn't you stop me?" he asked me one morning after he had slammed my face into the post on my canopy bed that resulted in my tooth going through my bottom lip the night before. He saw my bruised, swollen face and busted lip, and rather than apologize, he had the audacity to ask why I didn't stop him? A fourteen-year-old kid stop a 200-plus-pound drunk man? Really!

Another time, he gave me two hundred dollars to go shopping after an incident. Like that would make the pain go away. There's still a knot of scar tissue in my bottom lip, but the emotional scars left in my soul . . . Money and stuff didn't take those away.

The day my father moved out, I couldn't even pretend I wasn't happy because I was thrilled. He had apparently been going to some kind of treatment program Monday through Friday, eight to five. Then, he'd go run one of the restaurants in the evening—well, that's what he said he was doing anyway. Then, one night, he woke my mom up and just told her he was moving out, and that she was going to have to get a job.

I found out the following morning when I was getting ready to go to school. My mother told me he wasn't going to be giving her much money. So that day, I got off the school bus downtown, applied for, and was hired as a full-time pharmacy technician. I called my mom right afterward and promised that I'd finish school because I still wanted to go to college. Plus, I just didn't want to be dependent on a man for my survival like she seemed to be.

She had met and married my father right after she graduated from high school. She was only seventeen. My father was in the air force and stationed in Sumter, South Carolina. Prior to my father joining the air force, I guess he and his two younger brothers had formed a band, so I didn't understand how he couldn't understand my desire to at least go to college and try to learn how to make a living in the arts. I wanted to be happy, not rich and miserable like he seemed to be.

The story goes that my father and his brothers were gigging at some party that my mother had gone to. She didn't have her glasses on and couldn't see, but my father claimed "she was making eyes with me," and a week later, my parents eloped and took off back to South Carolina. My grandparents apparently disowned her for a while and suspected that she had gotten pregnant. They had hopes for my mother becoming a nun, and her eloping with my father crushed that dream. And now here she was in an alcoholic abusive relationship with no college education and limited transferable skills.

Not only did I want more for me, but I wanted more for my mom too. In the meantime, I didn't mind helping her out financially. I really liked working at the pharmacy. I gave my mother most of the money that I made to buy groceries, pay some bills, and went to school in the evenings to finish high school. After I had completed night school, I was eligible to receive a diploma from my high school, but discovered that wasn't going to happen either. There was apparently a lien on our house for tuition that had been owed to my high school, and until that was paid, there would be no diploma. I was pissed and complained to my mother thinking that without my physical diploma, I couldn't get into college.

Then, one day, I came home from work, and my father's car was in the driveway. When I walked into the house, he and my mom were sitting at the kitchen table together. I remember standing there staring at them enraged, and they were both smiling. Then, my father turned to me and announced, "I'm sending you and your mother to real estate school."

Real estate school! What? Are you fucking kidding me? Of course, I never said that out loud for fear of reprisal, but I'm sure the look on my face was why my mom jumped in right away trying to sell me on the idea of how much fun it would be and how it was in the evenings so I could keep my job at the pharmacy.

Once again, I had felt like what I thought, wanted, was interested in didn't matter, and I went to fucking real estate school.

I failed the Wisconsin broker's test. I needed a 75 percent to pass, but only received a 73 percent. Of course, my father was upset about that too, but I wasn't. I never did find out what my mom received on her test. I'm not sure she even took the state and universal exams now that I think about it. Once she had my dad back and was moving to Florida, she didn't need a job anymore, and that's when I was sent to go work at our Green Bay restaurant.

Continuing to write in my journal, I digressed frequently and wrote. "Shit! I just realized that's probably why he sent me to the Green Bay store because he didn't have anyone to run it if he moved to Florida. That's why he kept his bimbo around too. His brothers were too far away running other restaurants . . . Fucking asshole! I hate falling asleep with this shit still on my mind . . . I need some new thoughts to fall asleep to!"

Jack of All Questions

When I woke up Monday morning, I jumped up, made my bed, showered, practically ran to the common room to eat, and shoveled breakfast into my mouth with just enough time before group to sneak over to Linda's office. We weren't supposed to go down the hall to the counselors' offices unless we had a pass to do so or unless the counselors came and got us.

Ignoring the rules, I quickly walked down the counselor hallway. Her door was closed, and her Do Not Disturb sign was hanging on the door.

I made it back in time for our first group and knew that we'd have a fifteen-minute break between the first group and the next one from 9:45 to 10:00 AM. I figured that would give me enough time to try one more time.

I felt like a kid waiting for recess and kept looking at the clock. As soon as we were dismissed, I took off for Linda's office again.

I could see light streaming into the hall from Jack's doorway. I'd have to get past Jack's office to get to Linda's office.

Jack was this long-haired salt-and-pepper bearded hippie dude counselor. He wore a tie that was never really tied, but just kind of just hung there clashing with his brightly colored hawaiian shirts. He wore John Lennon–type glasses and waved his arms around with excitement when he spoke. He always smelled good, earthy, like he wore some kind of natural oil that he got from some hippie head shop. He reminded me of one of those guys that probably attended Woodstock, did his fair share of LSD and shrooms and that one could lose track of time with while engrossed in deep philosophical conversations. He was extremely intelligent, but looked and dressed like a burnout beach bum. He ran the late-afternoon group therapy sessions, and I think he did some groups or something over at the Residential House too. His groups were my favorite. I found them intellectually stimulating, and they made sense. Plus, he swore openly, and I just thought that was cool—he was keepin' it real.

Rather than sneak past his office, I just strutted right by, like I was supposed to be going to Linda's office.

Her door was *still* closed, and her Do Not Disturb sign was still hanging there.

I was turning around, sighing and probably looking like a crazed caged animal looking for an escape, when Jack suddenly appeared in his doorway.

"Aren't you supposed to be in group right now, Kim?"

"Do you know if Linda's here today?"

"Hmm, answering my question with a question, huh?"

Sighing, but with only a slight eye roll, I played along, "Did I?"

"Oh, so you want to play this game?" he kind of smirked.

"What game?" I played back.

"Oh, you think I'm finished?" he asked.

"Well, are you?" I giggled with a raised eyebrow.

"Let's try this again. Aren't you supposed to be in group right now, Kim?"

"Well, yeah, but—"

"Yeah, but?" he interrupted. "We just talked about 'yeah butting' yesterday, didn't we?"

"I thought we were finished playing, aren't we?" I questioned back.

"Are you ready to answer my first question?" He had a full-on smile now that his mustache couldn't even cover.

"Yes, I am supposed to be in group at ten, but it's not ten yet, is it?"

"Then, what are you doing in the hallway looking frantic?"

So I did look like a crazed caged animal looking for an escape—jeez! I thought to myself, and I didn't know if we were still playing "I'm going to answer your question with a question" game, but I really *did want to know* . . .

"I don't know if I'm sleeping on the streets tonight, or if I get to go to the Residential House today," I responded.

"What did Linda tell you when you last spoke?" he asked.

Really? Another question! "She told me that she'd let me know by the end of the day today."

"And do you know what time it is?"

"No, do you have the time?" I chuckled, back to playing the game.

Looking at his watch, he replied, "It's three minutes after ten, Kim. Have you heard the term *'Let go and let God'* yet? Or how *'addicts want what they want, when they want it'*? Or *'acceptance'*?"

"Yeah." I couldn't tell if Jack was still playing, but I'm sure he wanted to, and he had already won. Jack was also one of those guys that could see right through anyone's bullshit. He may have looked and dressed like a hippie burnout, but he knew about this addiction stuff. All of the staff seemed to, and I couldn't help but wonder if they were all in recovery themselves.

"Have you begun working on the second or third step yet?"

"No."

"Have you even picked up your Big Book and read any of it yet?"

"Yes. I actually have," I answered with a little bit of pride.

"Well, that's wonderful, Kim. I have a great story for you to read. It's called 'Doctor, Alcoholic, Addict,' and I'd personally like to ask you to read it and then let me know what you think of the story—particularly page 449. Would you be *willing* to do that?"

And he ended that with yet another question . . . *Hey. That's the story I read this past weekend,* I thought to myself. There was no way I could remember a specific page and wondered how these counselors and recovery people knew what pages things were on.

So I responded, "I'd be happy to do that for you."

"Oh, you're not doing it *for me!* You're doing it for *you!* In the meantime, I suggest you get to group since it's started now. Here," he said, handing me a slip of small blue paper that had his name stamped on it. "Give this to Tom when you get back to group. It's an excuse for being late. Have faith, Kim. Trust in the process. It's not the end of the day yet . . . Acceptance of your powerlessness may just be the answer to all of your questions today."

"Thanks, Jack!" I said as I started back toward the group room.

"Hey, Kim," Jack called from his door, "maybe next time you have a whole weekend to fret about something, you could read your step packet and see how you might apply the first three steps to the situation?"

Smiling, I didn't even turn around to look at him, but raised my hand and waved the little blue slip he had given me in the air and giggled to myself while thinking, *Yeah, yeah, I heard you— another question . . . You win.*

Arlene

When I walked into group, Tom was in the middle of drawing more brain parts on the chalkboard. When he looked up and he saw me, I just held up my slip from Jack, and he gave me a nod. I was kind of bummed out that I had missed more brain information. I really found this THIQ (tetrahydroisoquinoline) that the scientists had discovered in the brains of addicts quite interesting, but apparently, they could only find it once a person was dead and had an autopsy. I wanted to know if there was a test of some kind that I could take to find out if I had this THIQ, but without having to be dead to do so.

When group was finished, I gave Tom my slip from Jack and realized I was really hungry. I'd search for Linda later. I had to eat first.

Everyone else had hurried outside to have a quick smoke before eating. I was feeling famished and was getting tired of bumming smokes from everyone. I'm sure they were tired of giving me cigarettes too, so I headed to the common area. A new girl in scrubs was sitting alone at one of the tables poking at the food on her tray. She looked really rough. Her hair was a frizzy, tattered mess. She had bruises all over her arms. She was really thin, and she looked pissed off, so I decided to pull a Frank and go introduce myself.

"Hi, I'm Kim. Can I join you?"

"Arlene. Sure." She barely looked up, and I couldn't help but wonder if she had just gotten out of jail.

"So when did you get here?"

"My PO just dropped me off a little while ago," she answered, stabbing her plate with her fork. "I was here a few months ago."

"Really, what happened?" I asked while swirling a piece of mystery meat into some mashed potatoes and gravy before putting it in my mouth.

"When I left here before, I thought, I got this shit! I don't need to go to any of those stupid-ass meetings, work their fucking steps, get a sponsor, and all that shit! I did pretty good for a couple a months," she said, continuing to poke at her food, but not eating any of it or making eye contact with me.

"What happened?" I asked while grabbing my glass of milk.

"My fucking boyfriend! He just pissed me off, and I thought, fuck it! Fuck you! I walked out the fucking door, went to the fuckin' bar down the street, and did a shot of Jack. I was going to leave right after that, but then, I thought, fuck it! That was really good. I'm gonna have me another. The next thing I knew I was walkin' over to the dope man's house. It was only a couple more days, and I was back hitting the pipe all fucking day and all fuckin' night. A couple days after that, I was sticking a fucking needle in my arm again. Fuckin' speedballin' and drinkin' fuckin' nasty cheap-ass vodka just to get to fuckin' sleep. God, I fucking hate this shit! I'm so fucking tired of this shit!"

"Did you go through the twenty-eight-day program when you were here before?" I asked, almost finished with my food while she was still stabbing hers.

"Yeah, but I just thought I could do it on my own. I felt so good when I left here too. I really wanted to do this, but I wanted to do it my way I guess. Hey, do you know who Jack is? The hippie counselor dude?"

Laughing, I said, "Yeah," as I was wiped my mouth. "I guess I'm not the only one who thinks of him as a hippie counselor dude," I said, giggling.

"Yeah, well, that dude knows his shit! If I had only done half the shit he told me to do . . ." she said, shaking her head from side to side. "Well, I can see y'all are done eatin', and I'll probably be puking before long anyway. I'd much rather be dry heavin' than puking up this shit. I don't want to keep ya. I know everyone likes to play badminton after lunch, so don't feel like you gotta sit here with my sorry ass. I gotta go do all the paperwork shit to get back in here again anyway. They just stuck me in here so they could eat. They know damn well I'm certainly not going to be able to eat for at least a couple days. I hate being dope sick! Fuck! Why did I do this again?" she kind of yelled and slammed her fork down.

"Are you sure you don't need to talk more or vent?" I asked.

"Yeah, I'm sure. I'll see you around though. Thanks for comin' over and talkin' with me." She looked up, almost making eye contact from behind her brown-haired mop.

Picking up my dishes to place in the bus tub, I couldn't help but think about how the tables had turned in just a few short days. I was thinking the same things about Arlene that I'm sure Karen was probably thinking about me, *Wow! She's pretty banged up, and she sure does swear a lot! She looks like death warmed over! I hope she makes it!*

I walked outside, grabbed a racket, and headed toward the badminton court while Arlene's relapse story replayed in my mind:

- She blamed her boyfriend saying, "Fuck it! Fuck you!"
- She didn't go to meetings.
- She wanted to do the program her way . . . I could relate to that.
- She said she lasted a couple of months before she was sticking a needle in her arm again . . . hmm.

I didn't want that to be me in a few months or even a few years, and I wondered, *If I didn't do the things that were suggested by the people in the program, if I didn't do what was suggested like Linda had said, would I end up here again? Would I end up in jail again? How would that affect my son? What if I had killed my mom?*

As I threw the birdie up into the air to serve it, I noticed the yellowish-colored remnants of bruises on my forearm and found myself grateful that they weren't from banging dope, and I wondered, *What the heck is happening to me? Where the heck is this attitude of gratitude coming from? Is this one of those mini mir-*

acles that Linda is talking about? But I don't want to have to do those steps, go to meetings, get a sponsor, and all that shit! I'm different from Arlene . . . I can do it on my own without all that twelve-step bullshit!

A-a-a-men

It was absolutely beautiful outside. White puffy clouds floated gently by, providing a break from the intense Florida sun. There was even an occasional gentle breeze coming from the gulf, a perfect day to play badminton. However, what we played looked more like a bunch of really bad ballerina's attempt to jeté, chaînés, and pirouette in our attempts to volley the birdie back and forth over the net more than five times in a row. We lost track of whose serve it was. We had no idea what the score was, although some of the onlookers laughing at us would let us know. Half of us were looking in the air for the birdie while someone was actually holding it in their hand. Others were having air guitar competitions while others were zigzagging through the rest of us trying to balance their rackets on their fingers like a basketball. It was hysterically funny and blew our minds that we could laugh so hard and had so much fun while *sober*!

Our morning group counselor, Tom, used our after-lunch badminton-ballet battles, as we lovingly referred to them, to explain how our brains were healing. He explained that there were pleasure centers in our brains that were suffering from lack of chemicals that we had been artificially feeding into our brains. He said that science was proving that playing, laughing, and getting physical exercise helped speed up the recovery process for our brains to heal. Of course, I found that very interesting, but for me, it was more about the hilarious antics. And I think those that watched from the sidelines had just as much fun laughing at us as we did at ourselves.

Laughing at ourselves was a new concept for most of us. It was much more fun to have fun than to be all serious about who was winning or who was better than someone else.

Waiting for Tiny (who probably weighed close to 400 pounds) to serve, he suddenly stopped and asked, "Who y'all lookin' fur Miss Linda?"

I turned to look behind me, and there she was walking right toward me smiling. I immediately told the crew I had to go and offered my racket to one of the onlookers to jump in and join the fun.

As soon as Linda got me through the door, she stopped me and excitedly said, "You're in, Kim! The treatment team staffed your case this morning, and we'd like to offer you a scholarship for our twenty-eight-day program. We have some paperwork to complete, but afterward, you can pack up your things and bring them on over to the Recovery House. You'll probably be just in time to have dinner with everyone."

Jack's door was still open as we made our way down the hall. He must have heard Linda and me coming down the hall. As we approached his doorway, he popped his head out and said, "Hey, Kim, do you know what day it is?" he asked, smiling.

"Did you tell her where I was?" I laughed and answered back with a question.

"Do you know what time it is?" he asked.

"No, do you?" I played back.

"I know it's not the end of the day yet." He smiled, opening his eyes really big and looking over his Lennon glasses at me. And we both started laughing.

"What's that all about?" Linda asked as she opened the door to her office.

"Questions," I answered, waving my hand in dismissal to just ignore it, and I followed her into her office.

She picked up her M&M's dish, offered me some, and then took a handful herself. "You realize that you are a miracle, don't you, Kim?" she asked.

"What do you mean?" I asked while we were both eating M&M's and trying not to speak with our mouths full at the same time.

"Think of how many times when you were drinking or drugging. Think of how many times you could have died or killed someone else, and yet here you are. Don't you think that's a miracle?" she asked while passing me a paper to sign.

She didn't wait for me to answer, but continued, "You're a survivor, Kim. There's a reason that you're here. I'd really like you to consider that . . . Maybe, just maybe, you have gone through everything you have, in order to learn and to grow, to come out of all of this to a life that has just been waiting for you. Maybe, just maybe, our twenty-eight-day program will be the catalyst or the miracle that you needed to discover an incredible life filled with passion and purpose. You do have a purpose, you know, Kim. And I don't believe it's to continue waking up in a jail cell, prison, or leaving your son motherless because you overdosed or died in a drunken driving accident.

"People that come through treatment are given the opportunity to be exposed to the light. Have you ever seen a star sapphire?" she asked.

"As a matter of fact, my aunt Elsie left one for me after she passed away. My mom hasn't given it to me yet. I doubt it'll ever be given to me now," I said while I continued signing and dating the papers she was passing to me.

"Ah, well, then you'll know the answer to this question. How do you get the star within a star sapphire to shine?" she asked.

"You have to shine a light on it," I answered.

"Exactly!" she practically shrieked.

"The star is always there, but it doesn't really shine until it's exposed to the light. You, my dear, are like a beautiful star sapphire that is being given the opportunity to be exposed to the light. This is your opportunity, Kim, to let the light of recovery into your heart and into your life. Beginning this new life of recovery, you have the opportunity to discover the beauty and brilliance within you, but it will be up to you whether you choose to let the light in or not. It's always *your* choice. Take advantage of this opportunity. Look for the mini miracles and the light that will be shared with you. You may not ever have another chance. People always have another drunk or high left in them, but they don't always have another recovery in them.

"That's it. We're finished. Do you have any questions or concerns before I take you over to the house and introduce you to everyone?"

"What made you use a star sapphire as an example? That was kind of freaky."

"Well, as you can see by some of the items around my room, I tend to believe in what some might consider more esoteric or metaphysical-type things. Did you know that star sapphires are the second hardest material on earth, second only to diamonds, and are formed under extreme conditions like diamonds as well?"

"No." I didn't know that, and I was curious to learn more. "Do you know the metaphysical meaning behind a blue star sapphire?" I asked.

"Well, if I remember correctly, the people of ancient times considered it a powerful talisman of protection for seekers and travelers. I see you as a traveler on a journey into the light, a seeker of the truth, if you will. You just need to know where the light is so you can sparkle and shine. Any other questions?"

"Will you still be my counselor?" I asked. I certainly didn't want to have to have a new one.

"Yes, I will be." She smiled in a comforting, motherly kind of way.

"Can my son visit me?"

"Unfortunately, we don't allow children to visit, but we do offer family group where you can invite family members . . . I can see the sadness that just washed over your face. You can call Gene from the pay phone in the house though. I know you miss him, and you're worried about him, but you also know that he's safe with your ex, and Tracy can come to the family groups if you'd like him to."

"Yeah, but I should probably call Tracy to make sure it's okay that he keeps Gene while I'm here."

"It's already been taken care of. When Tracy brought you in here, you both signed papers, so we could talk with him on your behalf. At that time, he expressed his hopes that you would be able to stay for more than detox, but we told him that would be completely up to you. I spoke with him Friday afternoon, before I proposed your twenty-eight-day additional stay to the treatment team, to make sure he was going to be okay with it, and he was quite happy about your decision."

"Really?" I questioned, rather surprised. I barely remembered anything other than dealing with the intake lady.

"Yes, really, Kim. Believe it or not, there are a lot of people that care about you and know that below your dis-ease, you're a wonderful, beautiful person. They want to see you succeed and to be all that you can be—to shine."

"Jeez, Linda, I'm getting all choked up again," I said as a lump grew in my throat, and I shook my head in disbelief.

"What other questions or concerns do you have?"

"I'm going to need more clothes, some female things, and probably some money to use the pay phone."

"We have more donated clothes over at the house than in the detox unit. You'll have a chance to go through them. There's also a whole closet full of donated shampoo, conditioner, feminine hygiene products, and Tracy did say that he would drop off some money for you too."

"You know, Linda. I still haven't gotten my period yet."

"Well, we do a pregnancy test on all females when they come in, and yours came back negative. Maybe your body's going through changes from being off chemicals."

"But I really wasn't doing any chemicals. I mean I drank and smoked a little pot mostly just on Friday and Saturday nights. I really did quit doing coke last October, and my period is usually pretty regular."

"Well, just so you know, I believe you when you say that you only drank and smoked a little pot."

"Thank you, Linda. It's nice to have someone believe me for a change."

"Do you think you might be pregnant?" she asked.

"Well, I was using some spermicidal stuff the last few times David and I made love."

"David? You'll have to tell me more about David during our next session. For now though, let's try to figure this out. Well, you usually have to go at least a week or two past a missed period, and it should be morning urine. When were you supposed to get your period?"

"February 5. The day I picked up my white chip."

Looking at the calendar, Linda thought out loud as she looked at the dates in my chart and on the calendar. "Let's see. You came in on Friday, January 30. Today's February 9, so you're four days past due. So the next time you should have your period is around March 5, and your new discharge date will be March 9."

"Hey, that's the day before my son's birthday," I said excited that I was going to be out for Gene's third birthday.

"That's wonderful, Kim. Well, how about this then. If you don't get your period by March 5, we can give you another pregnancy test on Friday, March 6. And let's plan to meet tomorrow around three."

"That'll work."

"Anything else?" Linda asked.

"No. I think I'm good. Thank you so much, Linda! Wait, who is paying for my treatment? Where does the money come from?" I wanted to know who to thank after this was all over.

"We're a United Way agency. So when people donate to the United Way, a certain amount of funds go to provide treatment for those who don't have health insurance or who wouldn't be able to afford it otherwise. We also receive a lot of donations from alumni, those who went through treatment here. It's one of the ways that they give back to others—the gift that they've received. It's what many consider part of their twelfth-step work."

Hmm, what was that twelfth step again? I thought.

And just like she was reading my mind, Linda quoted it, "Having had a spiritual awakening as the result of these steps, we tried to carry this message to others and to practice these principles in *all our affairs.*"

I was impressed that she could rattle off the twelfth step like that while also wondering why she had placed such emphasis on "all of our affairs."

I Am You, and You Are Me

Linda walked with me to my room and knocked on the door before we went in. "Come in," came a faint, scratchy voice from the other side of the door.

"Arlene, sorry to disturb you, but we're only going to be a few minutes."

Turning over in her bed, she recognized me immediately and said, "Hey, Kim, y'all going over to the house?"

"Hey, Arlene," I responded. "Sorry we're doing this while you're trying to recoup."

"You two know each other?" Linda asked.

"More than each of us probably realize," I answered.

"Yeah, me and Kim are going to be great friends," Arlene said, grabbing the garbage can next to the bed and heaving into it. "Sorry," she choked before heaving some more. "Good thing I didn't eat," she said through gags and then spitting into the garbage can and grabbing some tissue to wipe off her mouth and blow her runny nose.

It didn't take long to pick up my things. Everything I now owned fit into a brown paper grocery bag. Looking around one last time to make sure I had everything, I looked over at Arlene one more time. She was hanging halfway off the bed with her face in the trash can when I said, "Arlene, I really hope you get through being sick soon and that you'll be able to join us at the house, but if you can't come to the house, I hope I see you out there—at a meeting. We can do this, but not on our own."

71

"I'll be back to check on you before I leave for the day, Arlene. If you need anything, please pull the call cord for help."

"Thanks, you two . . ." Arlene managed before pulling the blankets back over her head.

Once we were in the hall, Linda asked, "So do you two know each other from out there?" Linda tilted her head as though motioning outside, to the nonrecovering world.

"No. We just met during lunch."

"So what did you mean when you said you knew her 'more than each of us probably realize'?"

"She's me."

"So you saw yourself in her?" Linda smiled.

"Not only did I see myself in her, but I got some great advice from her."

"She gave you advice?" Linda seemed surprised.

"Well, not really advice, but when she shared with me how she had been here before, how she had wished she had followed the suggestions of everyone here when she left and didn't, how it was only a couple of months and she was back at it. She said she was really tired and full of regret. It was great for me to hear and witness. Did I look that beat up and talk that foul when I got here? I know it's only been a little over a week, but . . . oh and not to say anything negative about her . . . I mean . . . Do you know what I'm trying to say?"

"I believe I do. It sounds like you're experiencing some M&M's, and when I heard the genuine care, concern, and hope to see her at meetings, I couldn't help but see you sparkling and shining a bit there, Kim."

"Thanks, Linda. That means a lot to me—to have someone believe in me. I'm still struggling with feeling like I don't deserve anything good to happen in my life. Like I don't deserve to be treated nicely, to be cared about or even loved. It's like I'm waiting for the ball to drop."

"Staying for the twenty-eight-day program is going to help with that, but remember, Kim, it's only the beginning! Getting clean and sober is the easy part. Staying clean and sober once you're back out there, and life happens, without following the suggestions that we give you here, you're more than likely to resort to old coping skills or picking up new ineffective ones like gambling, food, relationships, sex, and so on. Well, I don't want to get ahead of myself here, but these are a whole other area in which to explore as a person in recovery. In the meantime, allow the group to bring you into the light. Allow the people whose bowls are full to help you fill yours and remember to stay out of the dark. You can't sparkle without the light."

Kitty

That night, I had dinner with everyone at the house. They all seemed really comfortable with each other. Everyone pitched in for cleanup and asked if there was a particular job that I would like to do or one that I really hated and showed me the sign-up sheet. That first night, I took the trash out and emptied the ashtrays outside into the bags before I carried everything to the Dumpsters beyond the gate. It was a strange feeling being beyond the gate. I wasn't sure if it was there to keep us in or to keep others out—maybe both.

When I came back in, one of the women in the house named Kitty informed me that was her "real name" and that her prostitute name was Deborah. She laughed about how opposite that seemed, took me to a huge closet, and before opening it, she asked, "Are you ready? You can take anything you want in here. You can keep it or donate it back before you leave, but it's all free!" And then she simultaneously opened the bifold doors and said, "Ta-da!"

I was surprised that there were actually some really nice clothes, shoes, and even accessories. Some of the items still had tags on them from the stores that had donated them. Kitty dove right in, reminding me of the saleswomen that used to wait on me in the higher-end stores. She began grabbing and holding tops, dresses, scarfs, belts, and shoes up to me and piling them onto my arms to take to the room we were sharing.

Acting like we were long-lost friends that had just hit the jackpot and were out on a shopping spree, Kitty shared with me how she had been clean and sober now for thirty-five days and how wonderful it was. She explained how she had wound up in Miami turning tricks to keep her addiction going, but how she was from Sarasota, was planning on staying here, and hoped to see me at some meetings when I got out. She went on to share with me how she had been at First Step years before because of her drinking, but then started to smoke some pot which led her to hanging out with the "wrong people—again," and before she knew it, she was smoking crack and turning tricks to survive.

She was really open with me about her life and seemed excited that I was going to be her roommate even if it was for only a couple of more days before she would be discharged.

Next, Kitty took me to a closet that was filled with toiletry items. Again, she said I could pick out whatever I wanted and that I could keep whatever I picked, but these items I needed, to take them with me. First Step wanted to make sure we weren't using each other's razors, toothpaste, clippers, or tweezers and such due to the HIV and AIDS epidemic that seemed to be running rampant—particularly in the gay community.

That night, before I went to sleep, I wrote about Kitty in my journal and how grateful I was that she was so welcoming.

The next day, Linda stopped by the house. "So how was your first night at the house?" she asked. Then, right after the kind of small talk, if you will, she asked about my notebook.

The notebook had been in the folder that the detox lady gave me. I had been writing in it since my first night in detox when I couldn't sleep. After that, I carried it around with me everywhere. I didn't want anyone else to read anything that I had written in there. I needed it to be a safe place to record the thoughts, feelings, and emotions that kept me awake at night. Once I could get them out of me and on to the paper, I was able to fall asleep.

Seeing me carry that notebook around everywhere with me, Linda asked me if I would be willing to share some of what I had written in it with the group that she would be running in the afternoon.

I hesitated, but she assured me that not only would it probably be helpful for me, but that it would probably help the group as well.

Three O'clock Group

S prawled around a large kitchen table, I clung to my notebook as Linda opened the group asking everyone how they were feeling today. I listened as others shared, sidetracked by my fears of sharing anything from my journal.

I was afraid of what they would think of me and my parents. I grew up with a strict understanding of "do not air our dirty laundry," but Linda explained that until I took that laundry out to wash it, it would remain dirty, grow molds, and shared how molds can make everyone in a home sick. She went on to explain that by exposing it to the light, working on one patch of grime at a time, that eventually, I'd have clean laundry to work with, "and you know how good it feels to wear clean clothes or sleep on clean sheets," she said, and I did.

However, despite everyone else sharing some deep and heavy stuff, I was afraid to show others my soiled past. I was afraid of their judgment. I was afraid of their rejection, but then I remembered what Arlene had said about wishing she had listened to the counselors, and I agreed to share from my notebook.

Everyone was staring at me to see what I was going to do, and then Chuck, one of the residents, said, "Go ahead, Kim. You've heard some of my stuff, and you still like me." He smiled. And he was right. He did share some of his "secrets" as he called them, and I did still like him.

Letting out a big sigh, I flipped through the pages, took another breath, and read,

"I'm sick and tired of being should on! 'Kimberly, shhh, your father's sleeping. You should try to be quiet.' My mom would whisper, putting her index finger up to her lips. This was code for 'don't wake him up, or he might beat the shit out of one of us and possibly both of us,'" I explained and then continued.

"'Kimberly, you should just stop talking back. Kimberly, you should just cry. Kimberly, he's a man, and he was drunk. You should have gotten him out of the bar sooner. Kimberly, maybe you should wear something that doesn't look so provocative!' This is a sampling of the things my mom used to say to me after my dad would either beat me or do something inappropriate to me. It seemed my mom always blamed me for his behavior," I said.

"Keep going, Kim," Chuck encouraged along with nods of encouragement from other house members.

I looked back down into my notebook and continued reading, *"It was a frickin' tank top! I was a teenager! News flash! I have big boobs . . . It's not my fault! Yet she'd make fucking excuses for him when he'd walk around naked in front of me? 'It's because he was in the service, my ass! But it's* my *fault that he grabbed my boobs and tried to stick his tongue down my throat? And not just once but several times? He even tried to stick his tongue down his own mother's throat at that Chinese restaurant once, and everyone laughed when she hit him. What the fuck was wrong with these people? What the fuck is wrong with my family?"* I ranted and then started to cry.

As I looked up, I saw one of the women crying. Then, Linda's voice broke the silence as she asked, "How's everyone doing? Can everyone here keep going?"

There were nods and mumbled yeses.

"Okay, Kim, how are you doing?" she asked.

"I'm pissed!" I kind of yelled. "I feel like I have to figure this shit out."

Linda sat there for a moment as I stared beyond her, feeling rage that could no longer be contained or numbed with substances, and it scared me. At the same time, I knew Linda was a safe person to allow myself to feel this rage with, and by other members' tears, I knew that they got it. They got me. They understood.

Breaking the tension, Linda asked, "Are you okay to continue reading?"

Letting out a big breath that felt like I had been holding my entire life, I exclaimed, "Yes! Yes, I am!"

"Okay, then, why don't you just keep reading until you feel like stopping. Is everyone else okay with that?"

No one really spoke, but nodded in agreement that they were okay.

"Does anyone feel like they need to leave?" she asked.

People verbalized and shook their heads no.

"Okay, Kim, proceed."

I looked back down at my notebook and continued filling in the gaps that I hadn't written down to give Linda and the group the back story in between reading what I had written.

"'Let's Just Wallpaper' is what I titled this one. So one Saturday morning, I was still in my bed when my mother came into my room wearing yellow rubber gloves, holding a bucket in one hand and a pink sponge in her other hand.

'Kimberly, you should have left the bowling alley sooner. Didn't you know there was a snowstorm coming?' she nonchalantly stated, not expecting me to answer her. Wringing the sponge out, I sat up and watched silently as she tried to scrub off the blue stains that were now all over my bedroom walls.

"I had gotten a new pair of dark-blue jeans the day before, and no, I didn't prewash them," I said, looking up briefly at everyone. "I wanted to wear them that night on my date. I thought they made me look skinny, and with my short, stumpy, gymnast body, bubble butt, and broad shoulders to hold up my big boobs, I needed something to help me kind of look like all the other girls.

"Ignorant to the weather forecast, my boyfriend and I came out of the bowling alley to several inches of deep, wet, heavy snow, and it was still coming down. The roads were really bad. We were in Eau Claire, but I lived on Lake Wissota—a good half-hour drive to my house in normal conditions. When my boyfriend and I got to my driveway, I told him to forget about trying to drive up to the house. The snow was much too deep, and I was sure he'd get stuck. Trudging up the driveway, I saw my father's Caddy parked under the carport. That's when that instant flip-flop churning that I was too familiar with began in my stomach. I remember thinking, Shit! I wonder what time it is . . . Like that matters . . . I'm late, and he's home . . . Maybe he's sleeping . . . Why is he home? Maybe I can sneak in? Maybe he's not drunk? Maybe he'll understand that the roads were really bad . . . Who am I trying to kid!"

"So what did you do?" Kitty asked.

"I slowly turned the knob on the side door. I thought maybe I could sneak down the back hall, get up to my room, into my bed, and pretend I was there the whole time.

"I peeked into the kitchen from the back hall. I could hear the TV in the front room, but I couldn't hear anything else and thought maybe I could actually pull this off. So I slowly crept up along the edges of the steps, tiptoed around the perimeter of the landing, and crept up the rest of the stairs—to avoid any possible creaking. Then, just as I reached the threshold to my room, I heard him almost sprinting up the stairs.

"'Where were you, you little fuckin' whore? Who were you out fucking?' he screamed, his face red with rage as he grabbed my arm and yanked me toward him.

"Cowering and knowing what was coming next, I tried to explain, 'The roads are—' Smack! He backhanded me across the face before I was able to say anything more, and I fell to the ground. Pulling me up by my hair, he began throwing me into the walls, shouting and screaming obscenities while my mother stood in the hall and screamed for him to stop.

"And people have the audacity to say I have a problem? And I'm the one stuck in this fucking treatment center? I'm sorry," I growled through my clenched teeth.

"Are you okay?" Linda leaned forward again with a look of concern on her face.

With another deep breath and release, I responded, "Yeah. I hope I'm not scaring you with how angry I am."

The group members looked engrossed and nodded and said things like "no," "keep going," and then Linda said, "Oh, sweetie, you need to get this out, and I appreciate your concern for everyone else, but it's not your responsibility to worry about them. That's my job. This is about you, not us and not me. However, I have to share with you, that day that you told me about your mom's response, the day you missed the bus . . ."

"Oh, the day that Randy wrote I was a whore on the road?"

"Yes. That day, Kim. I have to tell you I am so grateful that you're sharing this with everyone. No wonder why you were so angry. You have a lot to be angry about. Are you ready to continue telling us the story, to keep reading?"

I nodded and continued, "Once my mother realized that the blue dye was not going to come off the walls, no matter how hard she scrubbed with her little pink sponge, she again nonchalantly stated, 'We should wallpaper. That'll be fun. Want to go wallpaper shopping?'

"'Sure, Mom,' was all I could get out before I flung my head back into my pillow and covered my head with the blankets.

"I wrote these things the day that I got here. I remember looking at the clock on the nightstand and couldn't believe that it had only been four hours since I had been released from jail. I couldn't believe that I was the one lying in a bed at First Step, and having the time to think about this shit only pissed me off more. And the wallpaper incident, well, it's been like the theme of my whole life. When horrible things happen, we'll just cover them up and pretend that they never happened. I need a fucking drink!"

"Wow, Kim! So the day you got here, and you wrote that, you felt like you needed a fucking drink," Linda restated. "Does anyone have any feedback for Kim?" she asked.

Chuck went first. "I think that may have been your coping mechanism. It really sucks to feel so powerless."

Kitty jumped in, "Yeah, and to have your mom try to make you responsible for your dad's behavior. Being here has really helped me to understand that the things that happened to me when I was a child weren't my fault."

Tiny then shared, "Being here is really going to help you with recognizing where you begin and others end."

"It will also help you to learn to forgive your parents. It sounds like your dad has this dis-ease too," someone else pointed out.

A girl named Brandy went last and started to cry when she went to talk. "I was that mom," she sniffled. I was drinking cooking sherry, mouthwash, and vanilla extract because I didn't know what to do anymore. I was too afraid to leave, and I had no skills to speak of. I finally stabbed my husband when I was drunk, went to jail, and now I'm here, and my kids are in foster care. It's a good thing that you shared that, Kim. I needed to hear it. I'm just glad I didn't kill him in my blackout."

"So you're right, Kim. Your whole family has been affected by multigenerational patterns of dysfunctional-coping behaviors. It often takes only one family member, such as yourself, to get a family help. The point of treatment is not a punishment. On the contrary, treatment is a place to educate and teach you healthier coping mechanisms. Treatment is a place to not only learn some new tools, but to get you to practice them, so you can take them with you when you leave here. Again, it's easy to stay clean and sober when you're in a protected environment like here, which is why it's really important when you leave here, that you go to meetings, get a sponsor, and learn to live the steps. They won't fix your family, but the changes that you make can influence them," Linda stated while looking at each one of us.

"Is that why you said 'in all our affairs,' with such emphasis on the word *all*?" I questioned.

"Exactly," she replied with those kind, motherly eyes. "We're going to work on as much as we can while you're here in group and in individual sessions, but I really want you to get as much as you can out of being in the house too. There's so much you can learn from being in treatment. I want you all to not only leave with a full toolbox, but to know how to use those tools when you need them."

Although I was afraid to share from my notebook to begin with, I was really glad that I had opened up to the group, and I noticed that I actually felt lighter and somewhat relieved afterward.

The House

I kept wondering when Arlene was going to come over to the house, but she never did. When I asked Linda, all Linda said was that Arlene had the basic tools to recover. She just needed to pick them up and use them.

Between the meetings with people from the outside, my one-on-ones with Linda, Tom's and Jack's groups, I was learning quite a bit about this disease, which seemed to stem from my disease. I still struggled with the concept of powerlessness, insanity, and the whole *God* word. Although I hoped that once I left, I could stick with this recovery thing, but I was scared. Out of everything that I had experienced in the past twenty days, I think it was the house experience that had the most profound impact on my life.

Being in the house with a bunch of other folks who were also trying to do this "one day at a time, just for today" thing, I couldn't help but notice what a diverse group we were. Under normal—whatever that is—circumstances, I don't think most of us would have even acknowledged each other out there.

We ranged in age from nineteen to sixty-seven. We were male, female, and one of us was a transgender person. He had spent his life feeling like a girl trapped in a boy's body, but who mostly spent her life feeling alone, isolated, and filled with shame about who she was on the inside, while her physical anatomy fought her on the outside. Eventually, she tried to commit suicide by way of an overdose only to wake up and discover she was still here and still trapped in a boy's body.

The house held fourteen of us. Some of us had never been to treatment before, and some of us were "frequent flyers" (people that had been in and out of treatment multiple times), but had survived their relapse to give recovery one more try.

We were IV drug users that preferred the rush of sticking needles in our veins. We were the "just crush it and let's snort it" people. We were the "let's cook it up and smoke it" people, the garbage can junkies that would take whatever was available at the moment. We were the drunks who only drank alcohol "because it was legal" and who before coming to treatment didn't even realize that alcohol is just another drug in liquid form.

We were injured souls who somewhere on our journey had experienced things that led us to seek our solutions in our substance(s). We were people who, when life was just too stressful, overwhelming, or even boring, turned to whatever would help us to feel different.

We smoked, drank, snorted, and banged to fill the void, kill the pain, to help us forget, and it often began with a "fuck it!" or "fuck you!" We were people who felt like we had found a solution in substances, despite the negative consequences we had experienced as a result.

Below the chaos and unmanageability most of our lives had become, we were just people like everyone else. We wanted to be accepted, understood, heard, and loved, but before we knew it, our continued use only exacerbated our pain and our shame.

Some of us landed in jail, strangers' beds, hospitals, and Dumpsters. Some of us had criminal records and histories, but we had all landed here—in this house, at this time, and there seemed to be some sort of divine order to that.

We became the family that many of us never had. We encouraged each other. We cared enough about each other to call each other out on our bullshit when we heard it or when we saw it. We offered each other solutions that we were learning from our educational groups, meetings, and previous attempts at sobriety, and yes, those steps!

We didn't just listen to each other, we *heard* each other; we *saw* each other.

Some of us were closer than others, but regardless, when we all came together, it was all for one and one for all. We were able to share things with each other that only we seemed to understand.

We found humor in things that "the normies" (what we called nonaddicts) would find appalling. We laughed at the insanity of finding nothing wrong with lying on the ground doing one eyeballers, looking for anything we had spilled, cooking it up and snorting it or smoking it. We laughed at the insanity of carpet surfing and smoking our drug of choice mixed with an assortment of fine vintage fur and lint.

We laughed at the paranoia of knowing the feds were following us (and in some cases they were), fixing the blinds just so, so we could see out, but so others couldn't see in. We laughed at our psychosis when we knew that those weren't really crickets out there, but the feds communicating via Morse code, so we'd think they were crickets, while trying to hide from the "shadow people."

We laughed about adding water to booze bottles thinking no one would notice, hiding cans and bottles in blackouts, randomly finding them later in the weirdest places and then blaming someone else for hiding our booze on us.

We laughed at the insanity of thinking we could deal drugs without becoming our own best customer and trying to convince others we weren't high while we slurred our words, nodded, and faded midsentence, wore long-sleeved shirts in ninety-degree weather, constantly scratched, or blabbed a million miles an hour, while sniffling and rubbing our noses.

We cried together too—actually in front of each other. Some of us hadn't cried for years, yet the majority of us had suffered from some form of trauma, abuse, and/or neglect. I was amazed how one of us could tell our story so matter-of-factly, and the group would have tears streaming down their faces. It was as though we had detached, disassociated so much from some of the painful events in our own lives, that it took the group to cry for our pain in order for us to feel it ourselves.

It was through the eyes of each of these strangers that we saw ourselves. It was through taking the risk to bare our souls to each other that we were able to have some validation and to realize that at least to each other, we weren't worthless pieces of crap. We were addicts! And below our dis-ease and our dis-ease, we were caring, kind, compassionate, loving, considerate, creative people that were so much more than the way society generally looked upon us! We just needed an opportunity to try recovery.

I had grown to truly care about these people, who less than a month ago, were strangers. I had shared things with this group of fellow recovery warriors—things that I was planning on taking to the grave with me, and they had done the same. There was no judgment about what we had done while we were using. Rather, we understood each other and provided empathy, encouragement, love, hope, and support to each other—that just for today, just for this next twenty-four hours, "we" could do this.

I ended up at First Step because I had nowhere else to go. I never would have thought that I would have ended up wanting this way of life, that I would want recovery, but I did, and I still do!

Jack's Assignment

From the *Alcoholics Anonymous 3rd Edition*, also known as the Big Book, I had copied the "acceptance" part word for word into my notebook from the story "Doctor, Alcoholic, Addict." (The title has since changed with the printing of the fourth edition and is now called "Acceptance Was the Answer" and begins on page 417. I highly recommend reading this entire story!) Here's the part I copied into my notebook that Jack suggested that I read and try to see how I could apply it to my life:

> *And acceptance is the answer to all my problems today. When I am disturbed, it is because I find some person, place, thing or situation—some fact of my life—unacceptable to me, and I can find no serenity until I accept that person, place, thing, or situation as being exactly the way it is supposed to be at this moment. Nothing, absolutely nothing, happens in God's world by mistake. Until I could accept my alcoholism, I could not stay sober; unless I accept life completely on life's terms, I cannot be happy. I need to concentrate not so much on what needs to be changed in the world as on what needs to be changed in me and in my attitudes.*

When I met with Linda to discuss Jack's assignment of Dr. Paul O's "acceptance segment," I couldn't limit myself to just that section of his story. The first lines of his story, "If there ever was anyone who came to AA by mistake, it was I. I just didn't belong here," kept me reading.

There were so many parts that I identified with. There were so many ways of looking at things that seemed so foreign to me before I got to treatment, and I loved the way Dr. Paul O told his story with such humanness, self-reflection, and humor.

Linda helped me to begin the process of looking at taking personal responsibility for my own life and acceptance of my own powerlessness over people, places, things, and situations. And finally, she validated that it wasn't just me, but that my family was sick as well. I really needed someone to validate that the way things were in my house was *not* okay. However, she wouldn't allow me to use that as an excuse any more either.

"Once you're an adult, you can no longer blame your parents if you want to stay clean and sober. It doesn't mean what they did was okay, Kim. It wasn't okay! But you don't have to live your life as a victim anymore! You must begin taking personal responsibility for what *you want your life to be!* Remember when you told me that you weren't sure if you wanted to stop drinking or drugging, but that you just wanted to be happy? That you wanted your son to have a good life, a different life from the one that you, your dad, and grandfather had?"

I remembered and nodded.

"Recovery will give you that life that you want and deserve. It will transfer to your son, and you will be able to look at his life and your grandchildren's lives and know that the cycle of abuse and dysfunction has *finally* been broken."

I knew she was right, but applying the things I was learning wasn't going to be easy. And I still had issues with that *God* word.

I Couldn't Stay, But I Didn't Want to Leave

As my discharge date loomed like a ticking time bomb, I watched people leave that I had come to care about knowing the statistics were not in our favor. In our educational classes about our disease, they had told us to look around. "Only 1 out of 10 of you will make it to one year of sobriety," they warned. That was a scary thought, but I was determined to be one of them, while hoping that my newfound friends would make it too. I wanted our group to be the group that proved their statistics wrong.

As I went to meet Linda to work on my aftercare plan, I shared the irony of how I had only come to First Step because I had nowhere else to go, but as the days were winding down, I didn't want to leave. I shared how I felt safe in an environment where others truly seemed to care about each other, and what a wonderful experience it had been for me.

"Well, Kim, you've done really well here, and I promise that if you regularly attend meetings, get a sponsor, and follow their direction, work the steps, and eventually live them, you can and will have a wonderful life! However, I need to talk with you about your aftercare plan. I'm recommending a transfer to a six-month residential program for you in Clearwater. They can help you with attaining employment, housing—"

"*What?* Clearwater? Six months? I don't understand, Linda!" I interrupted as I felt the tears welling up from my eyes. Since getting clean, it seemed I went from never crying to crying all the time.

"Kim, your pregnancy test was positive. You're pregnant."

Shocked by her words, I sat there stunned. I couldn't speak. Looking down at my stomach, a tear fell down my cheek, and I knew more tears were going to follow. And I was hoping that I was gaining weight because I was actually eating.

My thoughts raced, *What now? How would David react to me being pregnant? Where was I going to live? I have no money! I'm not going to fucking Clearwater! For six months!*

Standing up, Linda walked around her desk, opened her arms to me, and just let me cry as she held me.

"We don't have to figure this out right at this moment, Kim, but we are going to have to make arrangements with this new development. I'm concerned that if you don't go to this six-month program, you'll relapse."

In a fog, I walked back into the house. Chuck, who reminded me of one of my best guy friends growing up, immediately asked what was wrong. I could barely speak, and my chin began to quiver. Practically jumping off the couch, Chuck came over to me, put his arm around me, and led me to the big couch in the living room. Within ten minutes, it seemed like the whole house knew. One by one, they made their way into the living room and had something to say when Chuck told them.

"Now you have another reason to stay clean and sober," a new girl that had recently arrived said smiling.

"You're discharging in like three days? Hmmm, I have to think on this one," one of the guys said as he sat down in the adjacent chair.

"Did you call Karen? She's your sponsor, right?" Jeanine asked.

"You just have to turn it over and know that your HP [higher power] has your back as long as you don't pick up a drink or a drug."

"Oh, Kim, this is wonderful news, a clean and sober baby."

"Are you going to keep it, Kim?"

Some sat down, others brought me water, coffee, or offered to get me water or coffee. In their own loving way, each person tried to figure out a solution to my situation, other than going an hour away from my son for six months, and all because I was pregnant.

They hugged me, offered advice and suggestions. Then, Chuck handed me another tissue and said, "You know, Kim, I'm scheduled to discharge the day after you, and I'm going to Fort Myers. I could give you a ride to North Port. Maybe you could at least get your car from your parents' house and go from there to a meeting? Leaving a day early isn't going to cause me to relapse. Besides, if us drunks and druggies can't count on each other, who the hell can we count on?" Chuck smiled, shrugging his shoulders.

Gasping and sniffling, I looked at Chuck and muttered, "That just might work, Chuck. Thank you."

And a plan was in place.

The treatment team did not approve of our idea, but they did understand and brought Chuck and me into a meeting together with Jack and Linda to express their concerns, wish us luck, and to say that they'd try to touch base with us Monday morning before we left.

It was a tearful parting for me. I squeezed Linda and Jack, and they squeezed me back as I promised them I would come back as an alumnus to share my experience, strength, and hope with the newcomers like Frank, Karen, Pat, and the other "programmers" had done for me.

That Sunday night was an emotional and tearful event at the house. We had all made a pact that none of us would say goodbye, but *see you all later at a meeting* because that was our hope.

The house had a huge shindig for Chuck and me that included cards, notes, phone numbers, hugs, chocolate cake, lots of coffee, and a farewell badminton match that even the weekend house counselors joined in to play.

I should have been exhausted, but I could barely sleep that night. I was full of fear and excitement all at the same time. Like a hotel, Chuck and I were expected to be completely off the property by 11:00 AM, and I had two kitchen-sized plastic bags filled with clothes, shoes, and toiletry items to take with me—a huge difference from getting out of jail barefooted, braless, in shorts, and a camisole—and of course, I had my white chip which I was beginning to believe did hold some magical powers.

I Still Don't Want to Hear That *God* Word!

C huck and I were packing up his car to leave when Linda seemed to appear out of nowhere.

"Kim, I have something I want to give you before you go." Holding out a new journal, she also placed a bag of M&M's in my hand, hugged me, and whispered in my ear, "You can do this. I believe in you, and remember, you are a star sapphire. Stay in the light and shine!" Her eyes were filled with tears, and I felt the sincerity in her words and gesture.

Tears were already streaming down my face. "I wish there were some way I could repay you, Linda, for everything you've done for me," I said, fiddling with the bag of M&M's, but maintaining eye contact—something I wouldn't have been able to do before, knowing people could see right through to my injured soul if I allowed them to look into my eyes for too long.

"You can," she said and smiled. "You can pay it forward once your bowl is full." She smiled, kissed her fingertips in a blowing-kiss gesture, and turned to go back inside. "Stay in touch, you two," she said without looking back.

I couldn't believe we were actually leaving. Everyone was in group, and it felt kind of weird that we weren't in there with them. It had been more than a month since either of us had seen the world beyond the First Step fences. We had the windows down, and I think we were both just taking everything in.

"Hey, Chuck, does the grass seem greener to you?" I asked at one of the first traffic lights we came to.

"Literally, figuratively, or both?" he asked, looking over his sunglasses toward the grass at Marine Jacks.

"Literally," I said. "It just seems like the grass is greener, and the sky seems bluer than I remember them to be . . . Jeez, was I that messed up?"

Chuck laughed, "Well, I think it's only going to be greener from here on out, Kim. Maybe we should pray together before we get to North Port—for God's will for you."

"I don't know about God's will," I responded. "But my will is that no one's home, I can get in, grab some of my personal things, my car keys, and get the hell out of there before anyone happens to see me!" I smiled as I tried to keep my anxiety from freaking me out.

I had finished my first, second, and third-step packets to the best of my ability while I was at the house. In treatment, the steps hung on almost every wall. The people that came in from the outside to participate in the meetings referred to the steps as "the solution." But I was still struggling with the word *God*.

As soon as one of them mentioned God, my body and brain seemed to have an immediate adverse reaction: my eyes would roll, my arms would fold across my chest, my jaw would tighten, and listening to others seemed impossible as my thoughts would override whatever anyone else was saying while thinking, *Oh, jeez, here we go again! Religious freaks! Cult! Yeah, yeah, yeah, God saved you! Blah, blah, blah! What a bunch of bullshit! Why use the word 'Higher Power' when I know damn well you mean your punishing God! I don't even want to hear that word! I was able to stay for treatment because of people and their donations, not God!*

I wanted a concrete solution to my using, not some airy-fairy God floating around in the sky crap! I wanted to know how to be happy like Frank. I wanted to be rid of the shame I still felt for being alive, the guilt I felt for beating up my mother, for my past, for not being as good of a mom to Gene as I knew I could have and should have been. I wanted my parents to change and their forgiveness. I did *not* want anything to do with any God!

But then, Chuck started to pray out loud, and out of respect for him, I listened while I tried not to roll my eyes. After all, I knew Chuck's intentions were sincere and thoughtful. The least I could do was be respectful of his gesture. Tearing up after hearing his words, I couldn't help it when a semiaudible "amen" just came rolling out of my mouth.

Chuck drove around the block so we could scope out my parents' house. Stopping down the street, he put the car into park and looked directly into my eyes and with such kindness said, "God will always have your back, Kim, as long as you don't pick up. You're going to be fine. I'll go park next to your car, and I'll honk if I see someone coming. We can do this!" he said as he shoved a twenty-dollar bill in my hand and gave me a hug.

"I'll wait to make sure that your car starts before I leave. Don't worry, Kim. It's going to be okay. God has your back, and so do I." He seemed so confident, but my heart felt like it was going to pound right out of my chest regardless of Chuck's confidence in his prayer.

Hugging Chuck as though my very existence depended on him, my tears of appreciation flowed onto his shoulder as I thanked him. "I'll see you in the rooms, Kim," he stammered as he smiled through his own tears.

Running out of the house to my car, I threw as many belongings as my arms could carry into the backseat. Scrambling, I jumped in, turned the key, and to my surprise, the car fired right up. Looking over at Chuck with a huge smile on my face, he responded with a thumbs-up and a huge smile too.

I honked and waved as I turned right onto US 41. Chuck honked and waved as he turned left onto 41 and continued his journey toward Fort Meyers. I watched him continue to wave until his image slowly disappeared from my rearview mirror.

As I drove back to Sarasota, I found myself overwhelmed with feelings of gratitude for the counselors, the intake lady, for Arlene, Chuck, Kitty, and for all the people that I had spent so much time with in treatment. I hoped that Chuck would be one of those that made it to his first year of sobriety and that I would run into him at a meeting somewhere down the road. I wanted all of us to make it, but I also knew the sad truth—most of us wouldn't.

Kicking and Screaming

"We"

W hen I pulled into the parking lot, I saw a crowd gathered outside near the entrance of the YANA Club, and in the middle of the crowd, in typical Frank fashion, he appeared looking goofy as always, smiling ear to ear, his hands and arms flailing about with his mouth appearing to move just as fast. Everyone around him was laughing and smiling and looked like they were having a great time.

After finding out what Frank had done for my family from Karen, the night I picked up my white chip, and after listening to Frank share at least once a week at the First Step meetings, I truly wanted what he had apparently found in the rooms of recovery. Next, I just needed to learn how he did it.

Just seeing Frank had me grinning as I stepped out of my car and began to walk toward the building. When Frank saw me, he opened his arms wide and yelled, "Kim! You made it!" just like he had the first night he saw me in First Step, and he proceeded to almost sprint toward me. I opened my arms to hug him back, and he picked me up and spun me around. Releasing me, he kept his arm around me as he led me to the group that he had been laughing with and proceeded to introduce me to others that I hadn't met at the First Step meetings.

When we went into the building, Frank introduced me to even more people and offered me a cup of coffee. It seemed like Frank knew everyone in this program.

I really didn't want to have to go to these meetings, but I was also afraid if I didn't, I'd end up like Arlene. It would just be a matter of time, and I'd be back at the stove cooking up and smoking coke, at the bar, or the liquor store.

Everyone else seemed to know each other, and I kind of felt like the odd person out, so to speak. It sure helped to have Frank there to greet me and introduce me to others.

Then, I spotted Kitty. She looked awesome—still kind of hooker-ish, but her eyes were bright, and so was her smile when she spotted me.

"Move it, Frank!" she ordered for him to get out of the way to give me a hug. Kitty said she had gotten a job in a clothing store in the mall and that she loved it. She went on to share that she had told her new boss that she was a person in recovery, and that her boss had worked out hours for her to attend her favorite meetings.

"You have favorite meetings?" I questioned.

"Oh, yeah, girl! You are going to love this one. There's a lot of really good recovery at this meeting—and they have dances and parties here at this club. It's thee place to be if you're in recovery. Come on, grab a couple cookies, and come and sit next to me."

The meeting began just like it did in the treatment center, with the chairperson banging a gavel on the table to signal that the meeting was beginning. He introduced himself and asked if there were any recovery-related announcements. There were so many fun-sounding things going on in various recovery groups, I actually got kind of excited about checking some of them out. After everyone finished sharing their announcements, he said, "Okay, let's open this meeting with a moment of silence for those who still suffer, in and out of these rooms."

Then, different people read the twelve steps, the twelve traditions, and he began to pass the basket which he explained was to help with the costs of paying rent, providing literature, and hosting the group's parties and such. The familiar poker chips were sitting on the table next to him, and silly as it would have seemed to me when I first went into treatment, I now wanted to earn one of those blue poker chips.

Next, the chairperson asked if there was "anyone attending this meeting for the first time," and I raised my hand and introduced myself as an addict, and everyone said, "Hi, Kim. Welcome."

Since I was new, the chairperson decided that the topic would be for others to share how they were able to stay clean. When someone was ready to share, they raised their hand, and the chairperson called on them.

I didn't know if it was appropriate or not, but I took out my new journal that Linda had given to me and noticed that she had written in it:

"Dear Kim, May your bowl be filled with M&M's! Shine on, Linda."

Smiling, I flipped past the first couple of pages and took the following notes from that first meeting at the YANA Club:

- *When wondering how to stay clean/sober, remember honesty, open-mindedness, and willingness, that's HOW.*
- *This is a simple program for complicated people. Remember to KISS (keep it simple, silly).*
- *FEAR = false events appearing real*
- *Hungry, angry, lonely, or tired? HALT and get my ass to a meeting or pick up the phone and call another person in recovery*
- *This is a disease. Like a diabetic that takes insulin, I have to follow a recovery prescription, which is as follows:*
  1. *Don't pick up a drink or a drug no matter what!*
  2. *Regularly attend meetings!*
  3. *Regularly work with a sponsor!*
  4. *Work the steps!*
  5. *Read recovery literature daily!*

And then Betsy spoke.

Betsy looked to be in her mid to late thirties. She had dark hair that had a gentle wave to it and kind eyes. She seemed poised, classy, and had a gentleness about her that made her seem very approachable. When she spoke, it felt like the energy of the entire room had shifted, and I took note.

Looking at me from across the table, she spoke about her difficulties in the beginning with admitting that she was powerless over her compulsions, obsessions, and desires to use substances and how she originally thought she just had issues with a particular substance: "Like blacking out on hard liquor, but thinking if I just switched to beer, I could avoid a blackout. I was always trying to find the perfect combination of alcohol and drugs to take me to that place, but I always ended up in some stranger's bed, jail, passed out in my own vomit, or in the unemployment line." We all laughed out loud, and she continued.

"I just couldn't figure it out! The results that I ended up with were never the same as my intentions were. I was just going to stop for 'one,'" she said making quotation marks in the air. "And while I was busy judging myself by my intentions, the rest of the world was judging me by my actions.

"What I discovered was that it wasn't the tenth beer or the fifth shot that led to the consequences I experienced. It wasn't the whiskey, the wine, or the combination of drugs that I took, with or without alcohol. It was that first hit, that first snort, that first shot, drink, or drag. *It was always that first one* that set my disease into motion that resulted in the negative consequences that I experienced."

Betsy had my attention. I had never thought about it that way, and it made sense to me.

"*One* of *any* kind of mood- or mind-altering substance is too much for me!"

Continuing, Betsy spoke of how the solution for her was in the steps, but when she first came into the program, she had a problem with the word *God*.

Me too! Me too! I thought. And at that point, I stopped writing and just listened in awe of what she was saying. She was telling my experience, and I wanted to know how she overcame this God issue. If it had worked for her, *maybe* it could work for me.

"Someone shared with me the concept of using the word *God* as an acronym for 'group of drunks or druggies,' but to make sure they were drunks and druggies that were in the rooms of recovery."

I started writing again as fast as I could, clinging to her words and thought, *Jeez, there sure are a lot of acronyms in this program, but I have to write this one down. That was good!*

"I also thought 'I,'" she continued, making quotation marks in the air again, "could do this on my own until I heard someone in the rooms share that they hadn't developed a lifestyle of drinking and drugging on their own, and that if I wanted recovery, I was going to need others to teach me how to do recovery as well.

"The first word in each step other than the twelfth step is 'we,' and I have to remember that I can't do recovery alone either. Besides, who would want to?" she said rhetorically. "We're a lot of fun, and who else is going to understand the things we talk about and our sense of humor? And with that, I pass," she said.

Reflecting on Betsy's words, I thought about how I needed others like Randy to teach me how to smoke pot. I needed easy access to alcohol in order to drink it as a child. I needed my friends to teach me how to make a pipe out of a toilet paper roll, how to mix drinks, how to cook and smoke cocaine, where and how to find drugs, how to weigh and package them, etcetera. I had never thought about that before. Just being in that meeting, I realized that I had no idea how to do this program either. I didn't know how to live my life without using *something*.

If I could combine having the happiness that Frank had with the wisdom that Betsy seemed to have, maybe I could actually do this. Maybe I could make it to ninety days of continuous sobriety and earn one of those blue poker chips.

That first meeting, I realized, just like at the house, these people got me. And just like Betsy, I was going to need this group of drunks and druggies in recovery, the "we" of this program to teach me how to live a happy life without using *something*!

In treatment, people always talked about this "sponsor thing." They made a big deal about getting one and said if we wanted a happy life, more than just being a dry drunk, which I learned was like my dad—not using substances anymore, but still a miserable SOB, that we needed one of these sponsors.

The problem, I never bothered to ask what a sponsor was, what they were supposed to do, or how to get one. I wanted to ask, but I didn't want everyone else that seemed to know, that I didn't know. I didn't want to appear stupid.

I would have asked Frank to be my sponsor, but I had heard that our sponsors were supposed to be the same gender as us. I talked with Karen before and after the meetings at First Step, but I didn't ask Karen because I had asked her if she'd call David for me, to let him know that I was in treatment, and she said that I really needed to focus on myself right now and not David. That really pissed me off.

Now that I was out of treatment, and I wanted to make it to ninety days clean and get one of those blue poker chips, I probably needed one of these sponsors and thought I may want Betsy to be mine.

After the meeting, I nervously walked over toward Betsy. She had a small crowd around her, and I listened to Kitty while keeping an eye on Betsy. It was difficult for me not to run out the door and use the excuses that were going on in my head: *She's too busy! What if she says no? She doesn't have the time. Look at her. She's already busy with people . . .* I continued listening to Kitty and some of the others who were talking. Then, Betsy suddenly looked at me and gave me a nod like she was reading my mind or something as she started walking toward me, and the crowd that surrounded her began to turn their attention to other people.

"Betsy. Nice to meet you . . . Kim?" she asked, sticking her right hand out to shake mine.

"Kim. Yes, nice to meet you too," I responded, shaking her hand and smiling.

"You just got out of treatment—are you hungry?"

"Well . . ." I paused.

"My treat," she interjected and smiled.

I was pretty hungry, and so I responded, "As long as it's not at the Silver Star." And no sooner did I say that when Frank came over to find out if we would be joining them at the Silver Star. Betsy and I looked at each other, smiled, and simultaneously said, "No, thank you," and giggled.

"Rain check," he said as he reached to give Betsy a hug. "Take good care of her."

"Oh, I will," Betsy replied, still smiling.

As Frank reached to hug me, he said, loud enough for Betsy to hear, "She'd be a wonderful sponsor for you, Kim," and he kissed my cheek, looked at me, and said, "We will see you tomorrow then," as though it were an instruction rather than a question.

"I'm planning on it," I smiled as everyone began to disperse to their cars.

"Well, since we are not going to the Silver Star, I was thinking we could stop at this organic market that I love, grab a salad or something to go, and head over to Bee Ridge Park? You can leave your car here, and I can bring you back."

"That sounds great."

Bee Ridge Park and Betsy

Betsy listened intently and nodded in understanding as I told her how I had landed in jail, treatment, and then this first meeting at the YANA Club. She assured me that I was not alone and that as long as I followed the "recovery prescription" I had written down from the meeting, that even I could not only have sobriety, but recovery.

She went on to explain that recovery wasn't just about not using substances, but that it provided us with an opportunity to find our purpose and fulfill it, to have health and happiness in our relationships, our homes, and our communities—"a wonderful life!" is how she surmised it.

As I sat and listened to Betsy share the horrific details of how recovery had transformed her life from a divorce, bouts in jail, losing custody of her daughter, eating out of Dumpsters, and panhandling to get her next fix, to having a great job as a counselor, a great relationship with her daughter, a house, a car, and a wonderful life, I also noticed that she had a calmness, a spiritual presence about her, and I wanted that too, and I told her so.

"Working a program of recovery is simple, but it's not easy. You know those promises that are read at the end of the meeting?" she questioned.

"Yeah, I like those." And then took a sip of my juice and continued listening while I finished my salad.

"Well, those promises come after the ninth step." And then she proceeded to recite them off the top of her head: "If we are painstaking about this phase of our development, we will be amazed before we are halfway through. We are going to know a new freedom and a new happiness. We will not regret the past nor wish to shut the door on it. We will comprehend the word serenity, and we will know peace. No matter how far down the scale we have gone, we will see how our experience can benefit others. That feeling of uselessness and self-pity will disappear. We will lose interest in selfish things and gain interest in our fellows. Self-seeking will slip away. Our whole attitude and outlook upon life will change. Fear of people and of economic insecurity will leave us. We will intuitively know how to handle situations which used to baffle us. We will suddenly realize that God . . ." She stopped and interjected, "A group of clean and sober drunks and druggies is doing for us what we could not do for ourselves. Are these extravagant promises? We think not. They are being fulfilled among us sometimes quickly and sometimes slowly. They will always materialize, and this is important, Kim. They will *always* materialize *if* we work for them!

"You see, Kim, it doesn't say they will sometimes, maybe, kind of materialize. It says they will *always* materialize . . . How?"

"If we work for them?" I half-questioned.

"How?" she asked again.

"Oh, I get it. How? Honesty, open-mindedness, and willingness?"

"And?"

"And . . . after the ninth step?"

She had already impressed me at the meeting, and now this? And I asked her.

Betsy, Will You Be My Sponsor?

Betsy said she would be honored to be my sponsor, but that she had some requirements that I needed to agree to as her sponsee, and I wrote them in my journal:

1. Attend ninety meetings in the next ninety days.
2. Call daily—at least for the first ninety days.
3. Be honest and open with her.
4. Call before I pick up a drink or drug, not after!
5. Be willing to go to any lengths—if I wanted what she had. I had to be willing to do what she did and does. And she will never ask me to do something that she hasn't or isn't willing to do herself.
6. Get at least one woman's phone number at the next five meetings.
7. Ask them when would be a good time to call the following day, and do so.

This list was getting long and freaking me out a bit, and I didn't necessarily like women, so I asked, "What am I supposed to say to them when I call or if they ask me why I'm calling them?"

"You just tell them that your sponsor, and you can tell them that I'm your sponsor, is having you create a phone list of women in recovery. It's much easier to pick up the phone when you need to if you've already established contact with the person. Trust me. Keep writing your list, we're not finished yet," she instructed.

"8. Read the first 164 pages of the Big Book, highlight things that apply to you, and write down questions that you have, which we will go over when we meet once a week. And we will be meeting once a week for at least an hour."

Waiting for her to say something else, I looked at her, ready to write more, and she said, "That's it for now."

"That's a lot! I don't even have a place to live or a phone!" I whined. "I have so many things that I have to take care of first! It's my son's birthday tomorrow. I don't know if I can do this 'ninety meetings in ninety days' thing either," I explained.

"Well, if you don't have your recovery, and you don't put that ahead of everything else, you will either end up in jail, an institution, or a casket, but *the choice is always yours*, but if you pick up that first drink or that first drug, your choices are then going to be made by that substance and not you—that's the powerlessness part of the first step, you know."

I didn't know, and that was the first time I understood that as long as I hadn't picked up a substance yet, I still had power—I still had choices, but once I picked up some mood-altering substance, I would be powerless to make healthy, low-risk decisions that wouldn't land me in jail, an institution, or a casket.

"Once you're around the rooms for a while, you'll hear the stories of those who relapsed—if they make it back to the rooms. The first thing they always will tell you is that they stopped going to meetings, or they stopped following the recovery prescription, which of course includes going to meetings. Like I said in the beginning, this is a simple program, but it's not necessarily easy, but the rewards are so worth it!

"There are those too who you'll see come in and got a sponsor, but never called or worked with their sponsor. Then when their life feels out of control, instead of picking up the phone to work with their sponsor, they pick up the phone and call the dope man.

"There's a reason to follow all five of the items in the recovery prescription. They all work together to create the life that you want for you and your son.

"I know you said you wanted to earn one of those blue poker chips too, but I must warn you that during times of milestones in people's recoveries—ninety days, six months, a year and so on, many people think that they can handle a drink here, a pill there, or a couple hits, or just a line now and then. Oh, they may do okay the first time they pick up. They may even be okay the next time they convince themselves they can handle it now—use 'socially,' but before they know it, they're right back to using their favorite drug, and their disease usually takes off right where they left it or worse.

"Remember the results, however, will always be the same: jails, institutions, or a casket! So what's the first thing in the recovery prescription?" she quizzed.

"Don't pick up no matter what!" I stated, feeling rather proud that I knew the answer.

"But that is not the only item, if you want 'recovery,'" she said, making quotation marks in the air with her fingers like she had done in the meeting. "Like I said during the meeting, recovery is so much more than just not using substances. Recovery is about learning to create and live the life that you deserve to live, and you're not going to be able to do that if you're using!

"This is where the willingness in the *how* comes from. We have to be willing to put as much time, energy, and effort into our recovery that we put into our using. And for most of us, our using consumed our thoughts, our behaviors, and our lives on a daily basis."

I was writing in my journal as fast as I could, trying to catch every word she was saying.

"So what do you think? Are you willing to be my sponsee?"

"Yes . . . yes, I am, but I have all these concerns going through my head," I admitted.

"So you don't have a place to live or a phone. Would that keep you from drinking or drugging?" she questioned.

"No," I sheepishly answered, knowing it wouldn't.

"Well, then, what are your plans when you leave here?"

"I'm going to go to my ex-husband's house to see my son and ask Tracy, my ex, if I can stay there until I figure things out. I really don't want to live out of my car, but I guess if I have to, I will."

"Does Tracy use?" she asked.

"I think he may smoke pot once in a while, and he doesn't drink at home, just when he's out gigging."

"Gigging? He's a musician?" Betsy asked.

"Yeah, but since we had our son, he works a full-time job as well."

"So what are you going to do if he offers you a hit off a joint or a beer?"

"Oh, I don't see that happening at all. He's really wanted me to sober up for a while and wouldn't put me in jeopardy like that."

"Okay, but if something comes up, what are you going to do?"

"Um . . . not pick up no matter what?" I kind of questioned, unsure of what I'd do.

"How'd that work out for you in the past?" she asked.

"Not too well," I replied, looking at the long list in my journal, unsure if I could actually do this.

"So . . . ?"

"I'm going to call you?"

"And what if I'm not home?" she continued, reminding me of playing the "I'm going to answer your question with a question" game that Jack seemed to love playing.

"Get in my car and drive to a meeting?"

"And what if your car is broken?"

"Um . . . I have no idea," I said, looking to her for the answer.

"What's the recovery prescription again?"

"Um . . ." I stammered, flipping through the pages that I had written it down on. "Here it is . . . Number one: don't pick up a drink or a drug no matter what! Number two, regularly attend meetings. Number three, regularly work with a sponsor. Number four, work the steps! And number five, read recovery literature daily."

"Okay, so I'm not home, your car is broken down, and you find a half a joint on your ex's nightstand. Your son is sleeping, and no one would know if you just took a couple of hits off it. What do you do?"

Jesus, I had no idea she was going to be giving me all these directions and then fricking quiz me. Sighing, I finally said, "Work the steps?"

"And how would you do that?"

"I have no idea," I responded, feeling kind of agitated.

"Ah, now we're getting somewhere. Thank you for admitting that you don't know. *This is why having a sponsor and additional phone numbers are so important.* And when all else fails, you pick up recovery literature and/or something spiritual and read it to get through it. Do jumping jacks if you have to, but try to get a hold of another person in recovery and get your fanny to a meeting if you can. Do you have a white chip?"

"Yes, I do," I said, giggling as I pulled it out of my bra. "I guess I could always suck on this baby and wait for it to melt?"

"Exactly!" Betsy laughed. "Old-Timer Rodeo Bill?"

"Yep," I replied as we took a small laugh break.

"So what other challenges do you think or feel would keep you from following the recovery prescription?" she asked.

"Well, I only have twenty dollars, and I don't know how long I can last on that either. Regardless though, I want recovery, and I'm willing to put as much effort into my recovery as I did my using," I said, managing a weak smile, unsure I was going to actually be able to do it, while wanting to at the same time.

"Then, we're off to a good start!" Betsy smiled as she placed her hands on the picnic table and stood up. "So I can expect a phone call from you in the morning? Say eight o'clock?"

"Yes, ma'am!" I excitedly responded.

"You'll read some of the Big Book tonight?"

"Yes, ma'am!" I responded, feeling like a new boot camp recruit.

"And I can expect to see you at the meeting tomorrow at the club?"

"Yes, you can!"

"Great! Now come here and give me a hug." As Betsy embraced me, I felt a warm glow radiate through me that calmed me just as my fears of Tracy and Gene's response to me were beginning to resurface. As though she could sense my fear, she squeezed me a little tighter and whispered in my ear, "It's going to be okay, Kim."

I wanted to believe her, but I was scared.

"Just for today, the next twenty-four hours," she stated as she pulled away and placed her hands on my shoulders and patted them. "Come on, I'll take you back to your car."

Leaving the parking lot of the YANA Club, I felt I had made a good decision asking Betsy to be my sponsor, and she had told me that if for some reason, I couldn't stay at Tracy's, to ask if I could use the phone and to call her. That eased my fear a little bit as we waved goodbye to each other.

Reunited and It Feels so Good!

The shelled driveway crunched beneath my tires as I pulled into Tracy's driveway. Our dog Angie had her paws up on the windowsill and started barking. Then, I saw Gene's cute little face pop up next to hers. When he started happily jumping up and down, my fears instantly vanished.

Tracy opened the door smiling, and Gene came running out to me in his cute little pj's. I just scooped him right up, started to cry, and covered him in kisses while Angie jumped and barked happy to see me too.

Looking toward the door, Tracy was in the doorway smiling and said, "They finally let you out, huh? Come in. Come in. Well, you look much better than the last time I saw you." He laughed. "Sit. Sit. Can I get you something to drink? I mean . . . You know, I mean, without alcohol?" He wasn't used to having to clarify.

Laughing at his stammering, I replied, "I'd just love a glass of nonalcoholic unsweetened tea if you have one." I smiled as I sat on the couch trying to pet Angie and reposition Gene on my lap at the same time.

Tracy shared all the amazing things that Gene had done and was learning to do while I was gone. He seemed so proud of him, and I was proud of both of them. Tracy told me the whole story of going to get Gene. He said that he also went and visited my mom the day after he dropped me off at First Step and a couple more times in the past month.

"She seemed to be okay physically, but was really happy when I told her I had dropped you off at First Step and was happy that Gene was doing well too." He smiled.

"What about my father?"

"Well, you know how he is. He's just pissed and said he didn't give a shit that you were in treatment and that he never wanted to see you again, blah, blah, blah."

I explained to Tracy how nerve-racking it was to not only steal my own car, but how I snuck into the house to grab as many of my personal items that I could, while freaking out that my father would pull into the driveway up at any moment.

"Oh, he's going to be pissed!" Tracy laughed, seeming to get a kick out of pissing my father off.

Tracy offered me the leftovers from their dinner. We talked, played with Gene, cleaned up, and drank more tea while we filled each other in on our lives. He had been dating a woman named Nancy that he met while performing a couple of months before. He said she was really nice and that Gene liked her too. I was happy for him.

He filled me in on his family, his job, his gigs and new bands he'd learned about, but it was getting late, and I was going to have to say something to him soon, but then he asked, "So do you have a place to stay tonight?"

Gene had fallen asleep in my arms. He was sweating, and it was almost ten o'clock.

"No, and are there any plans for Gene's birthday tomorrow?" I asked, standing up to take Gene to his room and put him into his bed.

Tracy followed me and said, "Well, not to make you feel bad or anything, but considering the situation with you and your family, I was just going to invite my brother, Nancy, and a few friends over this weekend, have a cookout for a small celebration. When I spoke to your mom last week, she said she wished she could get Gene a gift, and I told her to just get well and that would be a wonderful gift. She told me she's going to be in traction another couple of weeks. Although I did promise her that I'd bring Gene up to see her again soon."

"Did Gene get to see her?" I asked.

"Yeah. I think it was good for both of them. Your mom cried," he said as I tucked Gene into his bed. Then we each leaned over and kissed our little boy on the forehead and then just stood there and stared at him for a moment.

"He's just so beautiful," I said as a tear rolled down my cheek and looked at Tracy.

"He's going to be fine, Kim, and so is your mom. It's just going to take some time," he said as he reassuringly put his arm around me. "I'm really glad that you stayed for the additional twenty-eight days." He double squeezed me into him for additional reassurance.

Sitting back down on the couch, Tracy turned the stereo off as though he knew a serious discussion between the two of us was about to happen. Taking a deep breath, I blew it out and said, "Here's the deal, Trace. I only have twenty dollars, a half-tank of gas. I have nowhere to live. I have to go to these twelve-step meetings to stay clean . . . and . . ." I took another deep breath and said, "I have something really uncomfortable that I don't want to tell you, but I have to . . ." And with another deep breath, I just let it out, "I'm pregnant with David's baby."

"Oh shit!" just flew out of his mouth. "Does he know?"

"No. I've been afraid to call him. He hasn't seen me since my last drunk. He has no idea."

"Well, you have to call him and tell him, Kim," he stated, almost shocked that I hadn't told him yet. "How far along are you?"

"I gave myself an approximate due date of October 28, but I haven't been to a doctor yet. The first pregnancy test they gave me was negative, but the second one I took was positive, so I must have gotten pregnant right before my last drunk."

"Are you sure it's David's? Sorry, you know, I just have to ask. No offense intended."

"None taken, and yes, it is his. I didn't have sex with anyone else. And yes, I'm sure of that." I knew he was wondering if maybe I had some wild sexual escapade while in a blackout, and I couldn't blame him.

"Well, since we're being honest here. I could really use your help with Gene. I've missed work a couple of times since you've been in treatment and had to turn down several gigs because I didn't have a sitter. If you stayed here, it would save me from having to find and pay a sitter. And in all honesty, I'd rather he was with you than a sitter anyway—well, now that you're clean and sober. He needs you. He's really missed you. Just look how happy he was to see you tonight. It would probably really suck for him to wake up and not have you here. Maybe we could figure something out, so you could stay here?"

"What will Nancy think of that?" I asked.

"Hey, you're my child's mother. That comes first, and maybe we could also work it out that I stay at her place once in a while too. That way, Gene can sleep in his own bed. I won't have to pick him up from a sitter after gigging at three or four in the morning or after I've had a couple of beers, and besides, he needs his mama. It'd be nice if Gene could *truly* have you here. You know what I mean—not under the influence."

I had never thought about that before, how I was there, but not *really there*, but I guess Tracy had and probably others had too. And I resolved that was going to change now too.

"Um, so you wanna sleep in my bed tonight? I mean alone . . . I mean you can have the bed, and I can sleep on the couch." He giggled a little and lifted his left eyebrow.

"Thank you, Trace, but it's no problem for me to sleep on the couch, but if it is, I'll let you know," I said, winking at him.

"Well, then, I'm going to hit the hay. I have to be up early for work. Just make yourself at home, and I'll see you in the morning. We can discuss any details about being roomies again when I get home from work."

Standing up to go to bed, I opened my arms to give him a hug, "Thank you, Tracy. You're a good man, and I really appreciate you," I said and kissed his cheek.

Tracy is a good man and dad. I really did appreciate all that he had done and continued to do for me. Hell, if he hadn't taken me to First Step, God only knows where I'd be right now or if I'd even be alive. I was truly grateful.

While Tracy was at work, I spent my days with Gene playing, going to the park, filling out and turning in job applications, going to meetings, thinking about David, and missing him. I usually had a dinner made, Gene fed, and bathed by the time Tracy came home, and then I would head off to another meeting *or two.*

It was a strange thing living with Tracy. I was homeless, jobless, and pregnant with another man's child, and we got along great as roommates and friends which I really liked, but it was also really sad. It was sad that we couldn't have gotten along like this when we were married. It was sad that our relationship began and ended as the result of drugs and alcohol, but we did have a beautiful little boy as a result. And Gene deserved to experience something different than I had growing up, and so did this new baby that I was going to be bringing into this world, and I intended to give both of them a better life.

Message in a Sandwich

W ith a sparkling boyish smile, he held the door open for the ladies as he walked into the deli. He was about six feet tall, had dark brown hair highlighted with flecks of sun-kissed gold, and his tan muscular frame looked yummylicious in his tight work shirt, shorts, and construction boots.

By the time he got up to the counter, I noticed my heart was beating faster, my palms were sweating, and I was trying to control an uncontrollable grin on my face.

Oh my, this man was hot! Keep your cool, Kim. Keep your cool! I said to myself as he flirtatiously placed his order. I wrote it down correctly, but I found myself completely distracted by him.

I had barely turned his order in when I found myself spontaneously writing him a note on my next guest check, *"Hi, my name is Kim. I'd like to get to know you better. If you're interested, please let me know."*

As the cook placed his completed order up, I slid the note under his sandwich and returned to the counter where he was waiting and handed it to him. "Thank you," he said with that sparkling smile.

When he turned to join the other construction worker at their table, it suddenly hit me, and my brain went into hyperdrive. *Did I really just put a note under that very attractive man's sandwich? What on earth was I thinking? What if he's married? He wasn't wearing a ring! Oh my gosh, he's going to think I'm a slut! What if he complains to my boss? Oh my gosh, I have to hide!*

I scrambled to the back of the deli toward the sink and nervously began to wash dishes out of the customers' view. I hoped that there would not be any negative repercussions for my boldness! But there was something about this man that just had me all shook up!

Then, one of my coworkers peeked around the corner and said, "Hey, Kim, that hot guy is standing at the counter and wants the rest of his sandwich to go, but he wants you to wrap it up for him," she said out loud, but then silently mouthed, "Oh my god. Hot!" as she turned away. I dried my hands off on my apron.

This was it! My heart raced. I turned the corner and saw him standing there smiling, all gorgeous with his plate in his hand.

"Yes, may I help you?" I asked, feeling my face flush while I tried to stay calm and come across nonchalantly.

"Would you be so kind as to wrap up the rest of this sandwich for me?" he asked, displaying that boyish, flirtatious smile.

"I'd be happy to do that for you." I smiled back, while I held my hand out to take the plate from him. Then, when he looked into my eyes and his fingertips feathered across my hand, I thought I was going to faint!

"I'll be right back with this for you." I grinned like a giddy schoolgirl.

"Thank you very much," he said.

Lifting the remaining quarter of his hoagie to wrap it up, I saw the guest check I had written my note on. Nervously, I picked the note up, unfolded it, and inside it said, *"YES!"* in capital letters and an exclamation point followed by his name, "Dave," along with his phone number.

I shoved the guest check into my bra—I didn't want to lose that! I took a deep breath and turned to walk back around the corner to bring him the remainder of his sandwich, and he was gone.

Love Was in the Air

David answered the phone on the second ring, and I began the conversation apologizing for my boldness and confessed how I had never done anything like that before. He laughed and explained that he was glad that I had taken the risk because he felt an instant attraction to me the moment he laid eyes on me.

"So what are you doing for dinner? Would you like to go grab a pizza? Maybe go shoot some pool or go bowling?" he asked.

"That would be wonderful," I replied. "But I have to tell you something first." And after a moment's pause, I said, "I have a son. He's two. He'll be three in March. I was married before." I just rattled it all off and then bit my bottom lip and hoped he wouldn't hang up.

"I love kids! We can take him with us if you'd like to," he responded. "Will six o'clock work?"

Shocked at his response, I excitedly replied, "Yes. That will work." I gave him directions to the house and ran to the room that I shared with Gene in my parents' house to get ready.

Feeling nervous, I wanted to wear something cute and classy, but not too dressy or too sexy. I didn't want to overdress either. After all, I thought he's a construction worker and probably drives a rusty old pickup truck. Regardless of what he drove, I wanted to let this man know that I was more than a deli waitress and that I wasn't just some cheap hussy that was going to put out on a first date—although I had a feeling that I might have a difficult time turning him down if the opportunity arose. There was certainly a strong sexual attraction between us.

Gene and I were playing ball in the front yard when this beautiful brand-new silver sports car pulled into our driveway. Looking up, I thought it was someone who was just turning around, and then he opened the car door. Like one of those sexy slow-motion commercials, David emerged from the silver sports car like an Adonis wearing black dress pants, a collared pinstriped shirt with his sleeves rolled three-quarters, shined black dress shoes, and that gorgeous smile. I was wowed and definitely underdressed!

After playing with Gene for a while, I led David into the house and introduced him to my parents. I needed to change into something a little less casual, and I invited him to make himself comfortable while I ran back to our room to change.

Gene reached his arms out for David to pick him up. Smiling, David slung him onto his hip and wrapped his arm around him. I was rather impressed by this. Just as we walked out of the front door toward the driveway, Bruce pulled in. And all I could think was, *Oh shit! I totally forgot I was supposed to go out with Bruce for drinks tonight!*

Bruce was a guy I had met at the deli too. He'd asked me out for drinks one night and then brought me back to his place saying something about how he wanted to show me his newly remodeled bedroom. I hated it when men just wanted to get me into bed—and on a first date? It just turned me off!

Bruce tried unsuccessfully two more times to get me into his bed, but I really wasn't interested in him. I really wasn't even attracted to him. However, he did have a nice car that he let me drive once because he was even drunker than I was at the time. He did have his own house, and he had a good job, so I kept him around as kind of a backup.

Excusing myself from Gene and David, I went to Bruce's window and told him that David was my brother's friend, and we had a memorial service to go to—we certainly were dressed as though it may be true. I apologized for not calling him to cancel our plans. He responded by saying he'd be back Saturday at seven to pick me up. Wanting Bruce to hurry and leave before my lie was revealed, I just said, "Okay," and started to walk over to David, who was putting Gene into the back seat and buckling him in.

"Who was that?" David asked as he held the door open for me to get in.

"Oh, that's Bruce. I forgot that we had plans tonight," I tried to say as casually as possible.

Starting the car, David asked, "So are you seeing him? Dating him?"

"We've gone out for drinks a couple of times, but I really have no interest in him. So where are we going for pizza?" I asked to change the subject.

We had a great time at the pizza place. We were a little over-dressed, but neither of us cared. After dinner, we went bowling, and my heart was not only warmed by David's patience and atten-tiveness with Gene, but by his classiness, his demeanor with the people that served us—and he was a good tipper too, another brownie point, having waitressed the majority of my life. He was such a gentleman. He opened every door for me and placed his hand on the small of my back to guide me. It really turned me on that there was such a wonderful, classy man behind his rough, tough construction guy exterior. David was like the total package, a manly man that could fix things, classy, funny, kind. Gene seemed to warm right up to him, and he treated me like a princess.

I found out the other construction worker he was with at the deli was his older brother and that he was the baby in their family. I discovered that he was a city boy from Detroit that had moved to Florida in 1982 to visit his parents, and like me, he ended up staying.

He was a great bowler and had actually won the money bowl-ing to purchase his car, but that he did in fact have a pickup truck for work also. He enjoyed golfing, playing tennis, and mountain biking. He had great taste in music. He liked the same genres of movies that I did. His parents had been married "forever" is how he put it. He had an older sister that had two daughters that he adored. He had never been married, had no children, and never lived with anyone either. He had a great sense of humor, was a classy guy with a great smile, and I really liked him!

Gene had fallen asleep on the way back to my parents, and I really didn't want the night to end, but we both had to work in the morning. Pulling into the driveway, David turned the car off and reached for my hand, turned toward me, and expressed what a wonderful time he had and how he had hoped to do it again soon.

Then, he asked—he actually asked—if it would be okay to kiss me good night. "Yes," I said kind of shyly while thinking, *Oh my god, yes!*

Leaning toward him to signal it was fine with me, he placed his hand on my cheek, and as our lips met, I felt a rush of electrical energy pulsate through my body.

Gene stirred in the backseat, and as our lips slowly parted, we gazed into each other's eyes in the soft moonlight, and David just softly said, "Wow!"

I felt the same wow, but just shyly smiled and looked down as I reached for the door handle.

"Wait, I'll get the door," David said as he opened his door, and the light turned on. "I'll carry Gene in too if you'd like me to," he offered with a smile.

After tucking Gene into the bed that we shared, David asked what I was doing Saturday night at seven. "Whatcha have in mind?" I inquired flirtatiously, wanting to throw him down on the bed and ravage him.

"Maybe we could do this again?" he whispered and smiled as he grabbed me and pulled me into him to kiss me again.

"I'd like that." I smiled, this time grabbing his butt and pulling him even tighter into me to experience the intoxication of his kiss again. I didn't want him to leave and felt kind of slutty having such thoughts on a first date. I knew that if we stood there continuing to kiss, touch, and rub on each other like we were, it would have only been a matter of a few more minutes, and we would have been ripping each other's clothes off regardless of Gene sleeping in the bed or being in my father's house.

"I'll walk you out," I said as I grabbed his hand to lead him to the front door.

"See you Saturday at seven then?" he asked as I closed the front door and stood there holding the screen door open.

"I'm looking forward to it." I smirked, thinking lustful thoughts. Smiling, he leaned toward me like he was going to kiss me one more time and then planted a kiss on my cheek. *What a tease!* I thought as I closed the door and floated back to my room in anticipation of Saturday.

Saturday at Seven

"Hey, Kim," my dad called from the garage. "Come out here!" My dad still barked out orders and expected everyone to jump at his command, and here I was a twenty-two-year-old divorced woman with a child still jumping when he barked.

David had just gotten into the house, and Gene had already intercepted before we said more than a hello to each other. Excusing myself to the garage, I gasped in horror as I saw my dad standing in front of David's and Bruce's cars with his hands on his hips, shaking his head from side to side in disgust.

Immediately, I had that knot in my stomach as I flashed back to times he was drunk when I'd get home from a date in high school. "What the fuck were you doing, you little slut! You're nothing but a fucking whore! You're going to be knocked up by the time you're sixteen!" His level of inebriation determining what would happen next. Even though he hadn't physically abused me in years, I found myself still always feeling like a scared little girl when I knew he was upset.

Taking a deep breath, I walked up to Bruce's window—he never got out of the car to open the door for me, and I just told him that I had lied to him about the other night. I told him I was sorry, but that I didn't think things were going to go any further with us anyway, and he just said, "Okay." And he just calmly put his car in reverse and drove away. My dad didn't say another word as he walked back into the house, and I was grateful.

After we dropped Gene off at the babysitter's, David asked, "So what was your relationship with Bruce again?" Apparently, David had looked out of the window and saw me talking to Bruce from inside the house.

Sighing, I said, "He was just some guy that wanted to get into my pants. I was never really interested in him. Heck, I wasn't even attracted to him," I flippantly explained.

"Then why even go out with him?" David questioned.

"I don't know. I haven't talked with him since the last time you and I went out."

"Well, didn't he see you going out with me and wonder why you were going out with another man?" he questioned.

"I lied to him and told him you were my brother's friend and that we had to go to a memorial service . . . I know that sounds terrible, and it is, but I didn't know how things were going to work out with you and me, so I didn't want to just tell him to take a hike. But here's what I do know, after I met you, I obviously forgot about him and that's why I told him to come back tonight. I did tell him tonight that I was now going out with you and that I was sorry, but I wouldn't be going out with him again."

"So the next time I come to pick you up, he's not going to be here to pick you up too?" David asked.

"No." I smiled sweetly as I leaned closer to him and ran my hand up his thigh.

Smiling back, he said, "And that's good enough for me."

Shit's Getting Real

After sharing with Betsy how I had met David and the way I felt about him, I sighed and said, "So now here I am, pregnant with his child, and I haven't seen him or talked with him in over a month. I went to Planned Parenthood, and they told me if I wanted to terminate the pregnancy, that I'd have to do it no later than April 19. April 19 is my mom's birthday, which seemed like a sign or something. Even if I had the money to do it, I don't think I could. My parents forced me to have an abortion when I was sixteen. Just like my dad called it, I was knocked up by the time I was sixteen. I got pregnant by my middle school/high school sweetheart, and I still feel horrible about having that abortion!" I reminisced.

"When's your due date?" she asked.

"October 28. I have a way to go yet."

"Have you tried to call David, to let him know?" she asked.

"No. I'm afraid of his response," I told her. "He asked if I had protection. I did, but it obviously didn't work. In all honesty, Betsy, I think he was planning on breaking up with me before my last drunk. One of the last times we went out, I ordered a shot for each of us when he went to the restroom. When he returned to our table, he looked at the drinks, threw some money down on the table, shoved his glass toward the middle of the table, and just said, "Let's go."

Seeing that he wasn't going to drink his drink, I stood up, and of course, I slammed both of them. I think he was getting sick of me wanting to either drink before or during our dates. He would drink pop most of the time and literally have one drink! I don't have to tell you. You know that one to us means at least three."

We kind of chuckled. "He's one of those 'normies.' I can only imagine how disgusted he must have been the night of my last drunk—so disgusted that he chose to drive away," I said, feeling sad and looking down at my belly.

"Okay, so let's get to work. You mentioned keeping Bruce around as a backup. What do you think that was all about?" she asked, cocking her head to the side and placing her chin in her hand.

"Well," I sighed. "I think it's because I didn't want to be stuck at home on the weekends. Bruce always paid for my drinks, and he always had some pot too."

"So you used him," she stated matter-of-factly, putting her arms down and sitting up straighter.

Sighing again and with a bit of an eye roll, while trying not to look at her, I muttered, "Well, yeah, but—"

"Wait," she interrupted. "You realize that every time you say, 'yes, but' or 'yeah, but,' that you negate everything you just said, don't you?"

"Well, no. Well, maybe. They talked about that in treatment. Well, okay, I do now," I stammered, still trying to avoid her eyes.

"Go on finish what you were going to say," she said, leaning toward me and resting her chin in both of her hands.

"Yeah, but many of the boys and men throughout my life used me," I said, kind of knowing that was the wrong answer, but also the truth.

Betsy would have none of that. She flipped the situation back to me and what my behavior was. "And so that makes it okay, Kim?" she stated rhetorically.

Oh shit. Betsy was serious! "No," I said as I leaned back, still not wanting to look at her or my behavior.

"Kim, I don't want you to feel bad about yourself. I'm just listening for your patterns, your way of interacting in this world. Just not using substances is not recovery, Kim. Awareness and insight into our patterns and then changing those patterns is what recovery is about. Recovery is simple, but it's not always easy.

"Unless we're willing to delve into our *underlying issues*, our *underlying intentions and motives, we're bound to repeat them* and not just by relapsing on substances.

"Many people pick up new ineffective and dysfunctional ways of coping: relationships, sex, food, exercise, busyness. Oh, the list is almost endless. *Balance is the key word here* and in all of our affairs. Not just as it relates to our substance use.

"This being said, it seems that when you've been powerless over things, you're either trying to control or avoid people and or situations which has left you feeling angry and fearful. And the way you've often coped with your powerlessness is . . ." Betsy paused, waiting for me to answer and reminding me of my therapy sessions with Linda.

"I've used mood-altering substances," I answered.

"What else have you used?" she asked.

"I don't know what you mean," I said, confused.

"Let me give you some examples," she offered. "Let's go back to what you told me about the neighbor boy, Randy. So you did things that you really didn't want to do *equals trying to avoid rejection*. You also *tried to control his impression of you*. You risked stealing booze from your parents *to keep from being rejected* by him equals again, *control and avoidance*.

"And what happened when you wouldn't have sex with him? He rejected you. I'm really sorry that happened to you. However, you also mentioned that you knew how to make that pain disappear and other painful experiences you've had by using avoidance—with drugs and alcohol.

"Now I understand he was your confidant, and that it was an out for you, *your avoidance* of your family's dysfunction. I get that, and we'll address that too, but for now, let's move on to Bruce.

"You went out with Bruce, a man that you weren't attracted to and that you thought was a pig, yet you lied to him on your first date with David. What was going on there?" she questioned.

"I was afraid of his rejection too. If things didn't work out with David, I knew I could call Bruce, and he'd show up. So yeah, if I get really honest, I actually used Randy and Bruce too."

"So were you controlling? Avoiding? Or both?" she questioned.

"Both?" I half-questioned, unsure if that was the correct answer.

Making small circles with her hand, she motioned for me to continue with the reasoning for my conclusion.

"I tried to *control* Bruce by making him think the next time we went out, he might get laid. However, I *avoided* him unless there was something that he could do for me: get me out of my parents' house, take me out and pay for drinks, get me high— avoidance?" I responded, still unsure if that's what she meant.

"Okay, now let's look at what happened with David. You didn't tell him on your first date that you were seeing Bruce or dating him, but dismissed him as just *some guy you had drinks with* that just wanted to get into your pants. What did you do to control or avoid the situation when David asked you about Bruce the first time?"

"I changed the subject to where we were going for pizza," I responded, still unsure if that's what she meant.

"You mean you manipulated the conversation to try and avoid his questions and control his thoughts?" Betsy asked with her eyebrow raised while she waited for me to answer.

And all I could think was, *What the fuck did any of this have to do with me not using?* I wanted so badly to just get up, tell Betsy to fuck off, and walk away.

Before I said anything, Betsy asked, "And the second time?"

I was pissed now and just blurted, "I told David that I forgot all about Bruce after he came into my life. That's the truth, Betsy. Hell, that's why he showed up at the same time on our first two dates. I totally forgot, or I would have called him."

"And?" she questioned, drawling out the word *and*, and she just left me hanging there, waiting for an honest answer to come out of my mouth.

"And . . . I probably would have made up some lame-ass excuse, just in case things didn't work out with David. Jeez, Betsy, I hate this shit!"

"I know this is uncomfortable, but you're being honest for a change! Go on," she prompted.

With a deep breath, I went on feeling just like one of those women that I hated, that only dated men for superficial reasons. "I also leaned closer to David and ran my hand up his thigh to distract him. Which translated to, I don't want you think about Bruce, so I'm going to try to *control you* in a way that I know will work so I can get what I want. This sucks, Betsy, and it's pissing me off!" I protested.

"Hang in there. One more, your mom. I know, I know, a touchy subject, but again, a simple program, but not always easy . . . so," she said, taking a deep breath. "You shared that you and your mom had gotten into a fight about you not bringing enough money into the house. You tried to control her, by winning her acceptance, love, and approval by getting two additional jobs. However, you've expressed that your whole life, as hard as you had tried, you felt like you were never been able to live up to your parents' expectations, right?"

I nodded in agreement.

"So to avoid your mother, your home, your dad, Randy's, Bruce's, and David's *rejection of you or to control their thoughts about you—as well as other things you're powerless over*—you used substances, lying, manipulation, control, avoidance, and all these things have made your life unmanageable . . . Hmm . . . maybe because you're powerless over people's thoughts, feelings, responses, etcetera?

"Now let me reiterate that I'm not dismissing your powerlessness as a child from your parents' abuse and neglect. I'm not referring to things *you were truly powerless over* like being placed up for adoption, being placed in the home you were, or anything that you were literally powerless over as a child just trying to survive.

"*What I am referring to is,* how you've functioned, how you've interacted in the world to try to avoid or control things that you were powerless over, the patterns and triggers that will send you back to the bar, the coke dealer, another man, to the donut shop, out for a new pair of shoes, etcetera—those things that may not kill you right away, but that kill your soul and your spirit in the process. And why? *Because they're only temporary external fixes!*

"Based on the things that you've shared with me over the last few weeks, it seems you have spent your life, up to this point, trying to avoid things that made you feel like, how'd you put it? 'Like a worthless piece of shit' while trying to control everything else. So it's going to be *extremely important for you to learn to be honest about your motives and your intentions for doing or not doing something.*

"In other words, *you've based your worth, your entire sense of self, on trying to control others' approval of you—or avoid their rejection of you.* Which by the way, you're powerless over.

"And when you've been unable to succeed at controlling them, you blame those people, places, situations, and things. Now you've just given yourself a reason to pick up a substance or substances to control or avoid your feelings.

"You see, Kim, *the real issue here is that you're not only addicted to substances—you're addicted to things outside of yourself to make you feel different—better—or to not feel at all.*

"You, my dear, have used 'screw it!' or 'screw you!' as a rationalization and justification to get wasted and all because you have been living your life from the outside in rather than the inside out!"

"Wait a minute, Betsy. So you're saying that because I was seeking Randy, Bruce, David, and my mom's approval of me, that's why I drank and drugged?" I asked, trying to understand.

"There's a lot more to it than that, but here's a quick summation of what I mean: It seems you didn't get the love, acceptance, and approval you needed as a child to develop a positive sense of self, and you have spent your life looking outside of *your-*

self for your sense of self. You've used people and things. Then, when you discovered those external things let you down because you had no control over them, you began using drugs, alcohol, people, and even more things to avoid your internal feelings of worthlessness.

"It may have been a survival thing to begin with, but it escalated to a point of becoming addicted to the substances that you used. That's why in the beginning of our substance use, the social aspect—using with our friends, partying, the feelings drugs and alcohol produce seemed to be our solution. We fit in, we had fun, and people liked us. We develop this false grandiose sense of self, until we crossed over into addiction.

"That's when our solution turns on us and becomes our problem. It's not about the socialization anymore. It's not about partying and fun. It becomes necessary just to function.

"This is why we have to explore the other things you've used addictively if you truly want recovery. *We have to get to your underlying motives and intentions—your honest motives and intentions.* It is time for you to thrive, not just survive! Does this make sense to you?" she asked.

"I think you mean like when I was a kid, if I was scared, I grabbed my blanket and my statue of the Virgin Mary to get me through a situation, but then when those things didn't work, I tossed them aside?" I looked at Betsy for validation that I was on the right track.

"Keep going. What else? Can you identify things your mom used?"

"Yeah, she lied, covered up for, and made excuses for my father. She gave us cues as to what to do or not do. She'd also feed us to try and make us feel better. I'm sure there's more, but that's just off the top of my head."

"And why do you think she did those things?" Betsy questioned.

"She was afraid of my father."

"Can you go further?"

"She was afraid that my dad would leave her, and she'd have no way to survive. She was trying to *avoid* being alone and penniless with no education, no job experience, and two children. And she tried to *control* how we felt by lying about why she was crying or by feeding us our favorite foods."

"Yes. That's exactly what I mean. You know, social scientists say that there are three ways that we become who we are: Number one, our observation of others. Number two, the feedback that we get from others—both verbally and nonverbally, and number three, the culture and environment that we grow up in.

"Now this is by no means to blame *anyone*! It's simply to gain some insight and awareness into our own patterns, the rules and roles that we have incorporated into our being and ways that we survived in dysfunctional family systems."

This was a lot to take in, and I wasn't sure that I was getting it all, but it was also making sense to me.

"So let's continue. Can you see how *your observations, the feedback that you received from others and the environment that you grew up affected other areas of your life*?"

"You mean like when something upset my mom? How I observed her taking Valium or making a Brandy Manhattan?"

"So you observed your mom trying to control or avoid her feelings by taking pills or drinking?"

"Yes, I did, but I never thought about it. That's just the way things were . . . This is getting intense, Betsy!" I stated, as light bulbs of insight seemed to be flashing through my mind.

"What type of feedback did you receive?"

"Well, it depended on what my father thought I did or didn't do or how drunk he was."

"So there was no consistency in your home growing up and life revolved around your father? There was also a prevailing feeling that no matter what you did or didn't do, that you were loved?"

"Well, they told me they loved me, but most of the time, I felt scared—and what I did or didn't do was based on fear, fear of his violence. I guess the observations and feedback that I received from my dad were always *avoidance*. Being drunk or working all the time and *control* by using fear, bullying, or money. That's probably why I felt like every time he bought me something or gave me money, that it was more like a payoff to keep my mouth shut or out of his own guilt *maybe*? My mom would tell me that I was being too sensitive or overly dramatic."

"So basically *if you weren't so sensitive or overly dramatic, you could control how your dad treated you?*"

"Oh my god, Betsy, yes! Or even how to avoid him by my mom shushing us so we wouldn't '*make him angry.*' One time, my dad had slammed my face into the post of my canopy bed, and my teeth went through my bottom lip. I had bruises on my arms and face. The next morning, he saw me and asked me why I didn't try to stop him. He avoided responsibility for my injuries and tried to control my feelings toward him by giving me two hundred dollars to go shopping."

"What did your mom do?" she asked.

"She explained that she had looked for me and had tried to find me before my father did. We were at a wedding reception at one of our restaurants, and I was dancing and felt sick. I went outside to puke with one of my childhood friends that I was dancing with, and he held my hair out of the way while I puked in the alley. He went and got me some water, and we sat on the hood of a car until I felt better. I guess my father was looking for me and because my mom knew he was drunk. She went looking for me too, but my dad found me as I was walking out of the alley with Rusty. He slammed on his brakes, jumped out of the car, grabbed me by my hair, threw me into the car, drove me home, and then well, proceeded to beat the shit out of me all the way up to and in my room."

"So in other words, you observed some dysfunctional ways of coping." Betsy used her index finger to point to fingers on the other hand as though using her fingers to count valid points she was making. "The feedback that you received was that *you were responsible* for your mom not being able to find you and *your inability to stop your drunk father from beating you up*—much

135

more than any child should or could be responsible for!" She shook her head as she pointed to another finger and continued. "So the observations, the culture, and the environment that you grew up included lack of any personal responsibility by the adults in your life who taught you that with pills, alcohol, or money for that matter, we can avoid or numb the truth." Now she was on her pinky, and if she had more points to make, she was going to have to include her other fingers. "Or with violence and intimidation, we can control people. Is this what you're telling me?"

"Yeah, I guess I am." Looking up into her eyes, I started to cry. "I guess my desire to feel liked, loved, and accepted not for what I did or didn't do, but for who I was or am, has been the underlying and driving force for . . . my whole fucking life!" I sniffled as my crying was nearing sobbing.

"Do you want to stop for today? How are you feeling below your tears?" Betsy thoughtfully asked.

"Empty. I feel empty and worn-out," I said, shaking my head from side to side as I looked down through the gap in the picnic table at the worn grass beneath my feet. "Just like this grass beneath my feet . . . Randy showed up right at the perfect time to tell me that he loved me because I didn't feel wanted or loved at home. Then, when he rejected me and that didn't work anymore, I begin to use substances more often. And I trusted people less with my feelings, so I could avoid being hurt over and over again. It's like my entire life has been a big lie based on what I thought others thought of me," I cried between sobs.

A faint loving smile appeared on Betsy's face as she reached across the picnic table to hold my hands.

"Like liking David so much, in part, because he made me feel worthy and deserving of being treated so nicely," I continued to blubber.

"And what happened there?" she pushed for me to go deeper.

"Eventually I let my guard down to see if he would still like me if he knew how much I really drank—if he knew the real me."

"And did he?" she questioned.

"No," I could barely respond as the tears were coming faster and heavier, and it became difficult for me to talk while gasping for breath.

"You're grieving, Kim . . . Let it out . . . You've needed to feel these feelings, and you need to allow yourself to grieve . . . It's okay," she said, letting go of my hands. She walked around the picnic table, sat next to me, and put her arms around me while I cried.

"What about your middle school/high school sweetheart? And Tracy?" she pushed, knowing these were buried patterns that had consumed my soul.

"Holy shit, Betsy, I get it!" I stated once my sobs were more manageable, and I could speak.

"I pushed and pushed for these men to prove that they loved me because if they thought I was smart, pretty, sexy, or whatever other positive thing, *then* I could feel good about myself. But if they thought or said negative things about me, that meant I wasn't good enough. I wasn't loveable. I was a worthless piece of shit.

"Then I'd push it too far to see what would happen, and *the rejection from them would reinforce my belief of being a worthless piece of shit!* Then, I could drink or drug or spend money, start an argument or whatever, and blame them for my misery."

"Bingo!" she excitedly said. "*And that is why we need to dig deeper into our patterns, our motives, and our intentions, my dear!*

"We need to discover who we truly are beneath our addiction, and most of us have no idea because *we've spent our entire lives being whatever or whomever some other person, thing, or situation wanted us to be to survive—to have some sense of ourselves.*

"The good news, Kim, in recovery, through following the recovery prescription, we get to discover *who we truly are* below our facades. *We get to become human* beings *rather than human doings.* We first have to admit our powerlessness over substances, people, situations, and things and realize that *when we try to control things out of our control, it makes our lives unmanageable."*

"The first step!" I interjected, feeling proud that I recognized it.

"Exactly, Kim. Do you know who you are without your parents' voices inside your head telling you? Or Randy? Or David? Or your son? Your employer? The guy at the other end of the bar?"

"No, I don't," I said, still sniffling and feeling like I was kind of getting it. "You know, now that I think about it, I think that's what was going on with my father too. His sense of self was wrapped up in how much money he made and how impressive his life looked to everyone on the outside. That's probably why he seemed so threatened by the truth. He actually hated the part of himself that was just like his own father. By being successful, by his definition of the word, it allowed him to believe his own bullshit . . . Ha! And to avoid reality, by trying to control it!

"Ah, pretty smart, aye, Betsy?" I smiled, tapping my head with my index finger.

"Do you need me to validate that you're smart?" she asked, grinning.

"No. Okay, well, maybe a little," I managed a weak-at-best smile back to her. "You know what though, Betsy, just saying that made me feel like I was being arrogant or something . . . There's this part of me that thinks I may be smart, but I don't believe it. Does that make any sense?" I asked, raising an eyebrow like she had earlier.

"Yes, it does, which is why you need to turn to a fresh page in your journal and write down your next assignment:

1. I want you to expand upon your first step, beyond alcohol and drugs. I want you to make a list of people, situations, and things that you're powerless over.

2. Next to these people, places, things, and situations, I want you to write how you've allowed these things to either control you or how you've tried to avoid them.

3. And how you have allowed these things to make your life unmanageable.

And then we'll meet again next week, same time, same place."

"Yes, we will, and I'm looking forward to it. Thank you, Betsy."

"Oh no, thank you, Kim. I needed to hear everything I had to say." She laughed as she put her arm around me and gave me a squeeze.

Betsy reminded me a lot of Linda. Maybe it was because Betsy was a counselor too. When she agreed to be my sponsor, she also said we were "starting with the first step." Originally, I was miffed and explained that I had already completed steps one, two, and three by the time I left treatment. Betsy's response to me was, "We never graduate from them, Kim. *We live them daily.*"

"One more thing, Kim, you may also want to reread those tenth, eleventh, and twelfth steps," she said. Betsy didn't care what I had done in treatment. I was starting over the way she had done it and writing it all out, if I wanted what she had, and I did. This was no longer about just staying sober for me—no! I wanted to experience the peace, love, balance, and genuineness that seemed to just ooze from Betsy's soul with everyone that she came into contact with.

What she was teaching me was that I could apply these steps not just to my drug and alcohol use, but to my *life*.

Working Toward
that Blue Chip

I continued going to meetings every day, and I hadn't missed one yet. Some days, I even went to two or three meetings, when I could bring Gene with me. Betsy had shared with me that there would be meetings where I would disagree with what others were saying, that there may be people there that I didn't like, but reminded me that these meetings were *for me* and *my recovery*. She told me to *"take what I want and leave the rest."*

She went on to tell me that some of the things that I might even learn was that I didn't want what some of the others had, but that I could use that too. "Principles *of the program* before personalities *within the program*," she said.

She also reminded me that if I went to a meeting where I felt like I had nothing in common with anyone, to *focus on our similarities rather than our differences,* and that if there were people that really irked me, that after the meeting and before I went to sleep, I should try to figure out what exactly it was within me, that I saw in them. She'd say *whenever I was pointing a finger at someone else, there were three pointing back at me* and that I should pray for them and for myself visually surrounding all of us with love and white light.

Surprisingly though, I really liked most of the meetings except when someone would bring their biblical beliefs into the meeting. Following Betsy's suggestions when that happened, I discovered that the meetings were where I heard how other people had gotten through difficulties and how they used "the program" to get through them without picking up some ineffective coping, control, or avoidance mechanism—whether related to their substance use or not. I thought it was pretty cool that the topics never seemed to be about drinking and drugging, but using the tools and the recovery prescription to deal with things that *everyone* has to deal with in life, but aren't fortunate enough to have meetings, sponsors, and a program to use to cope better with life.

I also discovered a meeting on Saturday mornings at Coquina Beach. There were a lot of young parents there, and they brought their children with them. Gene loved it. I thought it was pretty cool that our kids could hang out with other kids whose parents were in recovery. It was an open meeting, so the normies could be a part of our meeting too, and I needed to find a "home group." (A home-group meeting is where a person makes the commitment to not only attend that particular meeting regularly, but where they also sign up for tasks that help the meeting continue, e.g., making coffee, emptying and cleaning out ashtrays, setting up, tearing down, greeting people, etcetera.)

Of course, Betsy volunteered me to do things at every meeting we were both at. And if Betsy didn't, her sponsor, Ann R., would. Ann was my "grandma sponsor" since she was Betsy's sponsor and one of the people I was to call in Betsy's absence if I couldn't get a hold of her. Doing the volunteer work is how Ann and Betsy explained kept a person involved and as a result—sober.

The more meetings I went to, the more clean and sober events and activities I learned about and was invited to also. I was even beginning to develop friendships with other women, *and I actually liked them.*

At the end of each meeting that I went to, the whole group would always say, "It works if we work it," and I was beginning to discover that they were right. The biggest shocker of all to me, *I was actually having fun, feeling really good and basically enjoying my life without drugs or alcohol.* I would have never thought that could or would have been possible!

Golden Opportunities
for Growth

When I talked with Betsy Wednesday morning, I explained that I didn't know if I'd have my homework completed by the time we were to meet, and she questioned, "Homework?"

"Yeah, you know, powerlessness list . . ."

"Oh, you mean 'golden opportunities for growth' assignment," she responded.

Laughing, I repeated what she said. I liked the sound of that much better! Betsy seemed to have a way of putting a positive spin on things. I was looking forward to learning how to do that as effortlessly as she seemed to.

After the meeting, we left my car and went to Bee Ridge Park, our usual sponsor-sponsee hangout, and sat at our regular picnic table, and I read my list out loud to Betsy.

"So what are you powerless over, Grasshopper?" she asked using a 1970's television reference, which was about a Shaolin monk and his master, called *Kung Fu*.

"*Everything! I am powerless over everything*! I was actually getting tired of writing everything down. There were too many things! Then, it suddenly dawned on me—*I'm powerless not only over my addiction, but over people, their thoughts, feelings, responses, etcetera. And situations? It's the same thing!* And the more I tried or continue to try to control or avoid things, the more chaotic, stressful, and unmanageable my life becomes and feels."

"So let me ask you something. When you were a child, was it your aspiration to get drunk, fall down, or wake up naked next to some stranger? To black out and beat up your mother? To get drunk and forget Gene at day care?"

"No."

"And if you could control the outcomes of your using, wouldn't you have done so?"

"Well, yeah, I tried to—and for many years. I just never knew what was going to happen—"

"After I took that first drink or the first drug," she said with me at the same time while nodding. "It seems kind of crazy, doesn't it? Almost insane?" she added.

"And that's why I need to believe there's a power greater than me that can restore me to sanity," I said, smiling. "To think that I had any control once I picked up any mood-altering chemical is insane. To believe that I had any control over the outcomes or the consequences after ingesting a chemical is insane! To believe I could control my dad—insane! To control being placed up for adoption—insane! And then allowing myself to be controlled, angered, upset by the things I have no control over is like me being pissed because I can't control the weather—insane!"

"So now that you know that these behaviors, despite your best efforts, are pretty insane, are you willing to believe that a power greater than yourself, such as a group of drunks and druggies in the rooms of recovery can help restore you to sanity?" Betsy asked.

"Yes, I believe the group of drunks and druggies are the only ones who actually can, 'coz we get each other," I replied.

"So do you think you're ready to do your third step?"

"I believe I'm already doing it." I smiled sincerely.

"And what evidence do you have of this? How will you know for sure if you've 'turned over your will and your life over to a power greater than yourself'? That you're not still making men, your parents, and other things that you're truly powerless over your higher power?"

"I came to believe, and I made a decision to trust the people in the rooms—the group of drunks and druggies to be there for me in a meeting, to share their experience, strength, and hope with me. I have faith that the people in the rooms of recovery want what's in my best interest. I trust that they understand me like others don't, and I trust that I can count on them to help me stay clean, serene, and sober for another twenty-four hours."

"What does trusting these things do for your thoughts?" she asked.

"I have no worries as a result of my trusting," I exclaimed. "It's having faith that the God of my understanding has my back as long as I don't pick up a drink or a drug! It's living from a place of faith rather than fear, and my thoughts and behaviors reflecting that."

"And what is fear?"

"Fear is nothing more than false events appearing real," I stated, feeling proud that I now knew not just the acronym for fear, but felt I was actually understanding it and applying it to my life.

"And how does that manifest in your life? How do you know that you're living the third step?"

"I have an unwavering faith that as long as I don't pick up a drink or a drug, as long as I am working the recovery prescription for my dis-ease, I can have faith that everything is working out just the way it's supposed to."

"And what is your 'dis-ease'?" she questioned.

"My dis-ease is the result I experience when I try to control or avoid things that aren't to my liking—things I'm powerless over. When my life feels unmanageable as a result, my dis-ease triggers my disease."

"So now, say the Serenity Prayer."

"God, group of drunks and druggies in the rooms of recovery, grant me the serenity, peace to accept the things I cannot change."

"Okay," she interrupted. "What are you powerless over again?" she asked.

"Everything! Well, other than my own thoughts, feelings, and responses to something outside of myself," I responded.

"What about the slow driver in front of you? Do you have any control over him?" she asked.

"No, but I can choose to go around him," I replied.

"What about David's response when you call him? Do you have any control over his reaction?"

"Oh jeez, Betsy!"

"Hey, I'll say it again, this is a simple program, but the work we have to do isn't necessarily easy! 'We' have to work through the uncomfortable stuff, so you don't get the 'poor mes,' poor me, poor me, pour me a drink. Alcohol and drugs are not good for developing babies," she said and smiled.

"No, Betsy, I don't have any control over David or his responses. I'm powerless over David's response too, but I don't like it," I whined.

"And if you try to control David and he doesn't respond the way you want him to, your life becomes unmanageable?"

"Yes, Betsy, it does," I replied, not wanting to go there.

"So what do you have power over then, Grasshopper?"

Taking a deep breath, I replied, "My perceptions and my responses," I paused. "And I think that's actually about it . . . I think."

"Okay, continue the prayer now."

"The courage to change the things I can."

"Okay, stop. So you cannot make the driver in front of you drive faster, but you can choose to go around him. Is that changing the things you can?"

"Yes."

"Okay, so you cannot control how David responds or what he chooses to do or not do. What he chooses to say or not say. Are you powerless over him too?"

"Yes, but I still don't like it."

"Oh, you don't have to like it, but it's important now that you're in 'recovery' what you do when you're frustrated over being powerless. In the past, when you tried to control things that you had no control over and still couldn't control them, what were the results?"

"I'd get pissed and usually ended up drinking *at that person*, get wasted, and saying 'fuck it!'"

"So when people don't do things the way you want them to, how you want them to, and in the amount of time that you want them to, your life becomes unmanageable?"

"Well, yes, sometimes it still does, but I'm aware of it now." I breathed out slowly.

"Then what can you do to change the way you used to respond to the things that you're powerless over?"

"I can get my ass to a meeting, call another recovering person, read the literature, write, pray, scream out of frustration, listen to soothing music, run around the block, help another addict. There are all kinds of other things that I can do other than pick up." I smiled as I was beginning to understand. "It's my choice to decide how I choose to change the things I can."

"This is a great spiritual secret that many people have yet to grasp," she said, leaning forward and almost whispering like she had the secret of the universe, and she was about to share it with me. "Our thoughts, our behaviors, our perceptions, our responses, are *the* only things *we have any control over,* and *these are* our *responsibility!*

"The choice is *always ours!* No one can *make us* do or not do something, even if we have a gun pointed at our head! And no one can make us feel a certain way without our permission!

"It's *our* perceptions, *our* thoughts that make it so!

"Can someone else influence our thoughts, feelings, or responses? Yes! But it *is always within our power to choose* how *we think, feel, or respond*! We still have choices unless we pick up that first drink or drug. If we do that, we lose all of our options and choices," Betsy explained.

"So the wisdom to know the difference is realizing that I am powerless over people, the first drink or drug, situations, my ex, David, my father, my mom, etcetera," I kind of half-questioned.

"When you try to control these things, what happens to your serenity?"

"It's nonexistent, and my life feels unmanageable," I replied.

"Okay, so now say the Serenity Prayer slowly and think about the words you're saying."

"God, grant me the serenity . . . to accept the things I cannot change . . . The courage to change . . . the things I can, and the wisdom to know the difference."

"So how do you know that you're living step three?" she asked again.

"I know that I'm living step three *when I* respond *to life rather than* react *to it*. I know that I'm living step three when I have the faith or knowing that *everything is in divine order*. I know that I'm living step three when *my thoughts and feelings are serene*. I know that I'm living step three *when I have the courage to change the things I can* . . . 'Me!'" I said making quotation marks in the air.

"And *that* is the wisdom to know the difference," she said, clapping her hands together.

"Okay, let's go find a pay phone."

"What?" I asked, confused.

"You know one of those phones on a post, usually located on a corner or in a shopping center that people use to communicate sometimes?"

And all I could think was, *Oh fuck!*

The Dreaded Phone Call

As we drove toward the shopping center on the corner of Beneva and Fruitville roads, Betsy tried to assure me that whatever the outcome of the phone call to David would be, that "we" and the group of drunks and druggies in the rooms of recovery would get me through *whatever it was*.

"I just hate having to feel all these feelings!" I complained.

"Can you identify them?" she asked, briefly looking at me and looking back at the road.

"Yeah, I'm pissed!"

"About?"

"I'm pissed because you're making me do this!" And I knew right after I said "you're *making me do this*," that I was giving my power away, so I could make her responsible for my feelings, rationalize and justify my behaviors, and then blame her for any victimization that I perceived . . . All I could think was *Fuck!*

I hated that she had brought all this shit into my awareness! I didn't want to be responsible for *my* feelings! Not all the time anyway! It was so much easier when I could just blame other people or situations for my feelings, reactions, and my resulting behaviors!

Trying to backpedal, I rolled my eyes and made a dopey kind of voice and said, "Okay, damn it! You're not *making me* do anything . . . I'm agreeing to do this under your guidance because my own best thinking got me into this program. I asked you to be my sponsor, and yes, I trust your judgment. Blah, blah, blah. Okay?" I sighed and looked out the passenger window.

"Oh, was that a snippet of awareness and humility with a touch of sarcasm rolled into one that just came out of your mouth?" she laughed. "So you're angry with me, but what's below your anger?"

"I just don't want to do this! That's all! And you're not really giving me a choice right now, and I'm pissed about that too!" I crossed my arms and continued looking out the window and said my thought out loud, "I fucking hate you right now, Betsy!"

"What's below your anger, Kim?" she questioned again—almost insisting that I answer.

"Fear! Okay? I'm fucking scared! And I hate not being in control! Okay? There, I said it!"

"Of . . . ?"

"David's rejection . . . Having to raise this baby myself . . . Not having enough money to do it, being a single mom with two kids, with two different dads. I'm afraid I'm proving my father's opinion of me to be true—that I really am a slut! I'm afraid that I'll give up because I can't do it all on my own. That I'll relapse and lose both of my kids!"

"And what is fear?"

"False events appearing real, *but this is a real event,* Betsy!" I said even louder, feeling myself getting the familiar "fuck it, let's just get drunk, high, run away," and somehow avoid this.

"This event of calling David is real, yes. However, the unknown projections that you spouted off are false events appearing real. They're not based on anything but your fears and old tapes. What happened to your faith that you had less than an hour ago?"

"You know, Betsy, I don't even want to hear that shit right now!" I kind of yelled.

We sat through the next traffic light in complete silence. Then, out of the blue, she about scared the crap right out of me.

"Kim!" she yelled.

Startled, I uncrossed my arms, sat up, and looked at her. "*Be present,*" she said in her calming tone of voice. "*Be in the here and now . . . Look at how pretty the sky is . . . Breathe in that cloud. Float on it and just breathe . . . Just breathe in the beauty of this moment—right now . . . Know that everything is in divine order . . . Just breathe,"* she said, turning into the parking lot.

She pulled right next to the pay phone, shut the car off, leaned back into her seat, and took a quarter out of her pocket. Turning toward me, she held it up between her thumb and index finger and said, "We're going to say a little prayer before we do this, and we're also going to rub this quarter with blessings while we do. Are you ready?"

Huffing, I turned toward her, "Go ahead."

"Dear Mother/Father God, Universal Light, I know that you have Kim and this baby's best possible interests and outcomes planned for them. Please help Kim have the peace, serenity, and faith through this phone call. Please keep her and this baby wrapped in your loving energy and light no matter what David's response is—with a grateful heart—we thank you. Would you like to add anything?" she asked, holding the quarter out for me to take.

"No," I said almost crying, but not knowing why. "Would you come and stand next to me while I do this?"

"Of course, I will," she lovingly said, gently brushing a wisp of hair out of my face and behind my ear. "Let's go. Let's do this."

Betsy was already standing at the phone before I was even out of the car. When I closed the door, she picked up the receiver and held it out for me and said, "It's going to be okay no matter what, Kim."

Shaking my head from side to side in disbelief that I was actually going to do this, I put the receiver up to my ear, took a deep breath, dropped the quarter into the slot, and pushed the buttons to dial David's number. *Oh my god! First ring—clear! Maybe no one was home! Oh my god, please don't let him . . .*

"Hello," he answered.

Oh, his voice . . . I missed him.

"It's me, David. It's Kim." There was a pause. "Are you there?" I asked.

"What do you want?" he asked, sounding agitated.

"Well, I'm out of treatment . . ."

150

"So?" he cut me off. "After seeing you drunk like that, hanging half naked out of your bedroom window—in front of a neighborhood full of kids—trying to get me to climb in through the window . . . I sure hope you got something out of it! But it still has nothing to do with me!"

"I was half naked and tried to get you to crawl through my window?"

"Are you kidding me? You're going to play dumb? I told you that night that was it—I was done!"

"Really, David, I don't remember. I was in a blackout."

"You don't remember?"

"No, I don't."

"Bullshit!"

"I know that being in a blackout is no excuse for my behavior, but really, I don't remember, and I am so sorry! I'm truly very sorry, but I also really need to talk with you. Would you be willing to meet me somewhere? Please," I asked.

"No! I haven't seen you in almost two months, and the last time that I did see you, I saw enough!"

I heard his words, but I had difficulty believing him. I knew there was truly something special between us, and I knew that he knew it too.

"I have something I have to tell you, and I just think it would be more appropriate to do it in person rather than over the phone."

"Whatever it is, just say it. Like I said, I don't want to see you!"

Betsy gave me a nod.

"I'm pregnant with your baby. I'm due October 28."

There was a long pause, but it didn't sound like he had hung up.

"Are you still there?"

Sighing into the phone, he responded, "Well, let me tell you what I think! I told you the first night that we went out that the one thing that would end any relationship for me was to find out I had been lied to."

"Oh, I'm not lying. I'm pregnant with your child," I replied matter-of-factly.

"Well, I don't believe it's mine. You told me you used protection and that I didn't need to worry about it."

"I did use protection. Apparently, it didn't work though," I tried to explain while not being defensive at the same time.

"Well, let me tell you what I think. I think everything you've ever told me was a lie. Hell, you flat out told me you lied to Bruce. Why wouldn't I think that you'd lie to me too? And now you tell me that you don't even remember trying to get me to crawl through your bedroom window? How many other things did you do and with God only knows who that you don't remember? You know, Kim, I really liked you, and it's just too painful for me to see you. I have no idea if that baby's mine, and I'm not going to get sucked back into your web of lies, fall in love with you, and then find out you're carrying Bruce's or God only knows whose baby. So until you can prove that baby is mine, please just leave me alone! Don't call me anymore and just stay clear of me!" And he slammed the phone down.

Holding the receiver away from my head, my jaw dropped, and Betsy and I just stared at each other for a moment before I slammed the phone back onto the receiver . . . and then banged it on the receiver a few more times . . . and then I slammed it on the receiver a few more times.

"Are you finished killing the phone yet?" Betsy asked calmly.

"Really, Betsy? I'm f-u-c-k-i-n-g pissed! I really didn't have sex with anyone else, and he has the audacity to think that I lied to him! One thing I am not is a fucking liar!" I blasted while I stomped in circles in front of the phone. "Aaaaarrrrggghhhh! I fucking hate this! What the fuck, Betsy?"

Betsy usually responded lovingly to me, so I was really shocked when Betsy looked at me and said, "Oh, you're not a liar—really, Kim? Do we need to review your past? Your first two dates with David again? Lying by omission is still lying. Lying by manipulation is still lying."

"Well, yeah, but . . . Fuck! I can't believe I just said that!" I stopped myself right there. "I don't do those things anymore! I told him I went through treatment, and he knows damn well that I wasn't having sex with anyone else!" I retorted with my hands on my hips.

"Oh, so you've been clean and sober for what now? A little over sixty days? So the world should now stop spinning since it no longer revolves around you? You're clean and sober now so David should just do what *you want*, when *you want* him to even though you've been out of treatment for over a month and didn't call him? Just because you tell him that you're pregnant with his child, he should just forgive you and bow at your feet?" she ranted back, bowing like one would to a queen or something.

"Fuck you, Betsy! I'm not going to stand here and listen to this shit!"

I reached inside her car, grabbed my duffel bag, slammed the door, and started to walk toward her thinking she'd move, but she just planted herself between the car and the phone.

"Oh, so you don't like hearing the truth? You don't want to see how your behaviors have affected others? You're the innocent victim in all of this? And rather than admit your part in any of this, rather than use the steps and tools of recovery, you're going to just run away, avoid things you can't control like you always have?" she yelled back at me.

I stopped in my tracks and dropped my chin to my chest. "Fuck! Fuck! Fuck! I fucking hate you, Betsy!" I yelled as my duffel bag slid off my arm and into my hand. I shook my head and looked up at her, and she was walking toward me.

"So you hate me because you know that I love you enough to not let you get away with lying to yourself? Or because I see you and you know it? Or is it because you know that I love and care enough about you and that baby to call you out on your bullshit? Or is it because I don't want you to die from this disease?" she asked, opening her arms to me.

Dropping my bag to the ground, I practically dove into her, wrapped my arms around her, and through my tears, I sobbed, "All of the above, Betsy . . . all of the above."

Time

I ntellectualizing the steps, reading them, writing about them, talking about them was great, but the day I called David and didn't get the results that I was hoping for, I learned that actually applying these steps was definitely not going to be easy!

Betsy reiterated to me what Linda also seemed to drill into my head during our one-on-one sessions, that the twelfth step said in "all of our affairs," while reminding me that prior to that twelfth step, there were eleven others and that they were in order for a reason.

The twelfth step begins with the words, "Having had a spiritual awakening as a result of these steps . . ." It had me feeling like I may never get through these steps, let alone one day have the ability to actually put them into practice in *all* of my affairs!

I had almost ninety days of continuous sobriety/clean time. I was struggling with living the third step and realized that I either turn everything over to the care of my Higher Power and have faith that the universe *always has my best interest at heart* (even when things are painful) or recognize that I'm trying to force my will, which is what Betsy explained was another piece of my selfishness and self-centeredness. She explained that the selfishness and self-centeredness that the twelve-step programs talked about was when we thought we could control anything outside of ourselves. After the phone call to David, this insight made me realize that the majority of my entire life had consisted of trying to control or avoid what people thought about me, said about me, did to me, or avoid it all together.

Despite what had happened after calling David, I felt ready to try and call my mom, and I asked Betsy if she would be willing to do this with me too.

"Some things just take time, Kim. Have I shared with you the acronym for TIME yet?" she asked. Knowing that she hadn't, she continued, "Things I must earn."

"So what are you motives, Kim?" she asked, and I knew I was going to have to be honest, which meant I really had to dig and give Betsy everything and anything that I thought may be honest motives. Working with Betsy as much as I had, she would often say "wrong motives" if she knew I was trying to bullshit myself, that below the surface, I was trying to manipulate, control, or avoid something.

"I really miss my mom," I kind of free-flowed my thoughts out loud like Betsy had taught me to do. "I just really want to see her, hug her, smell her, feel her, and tell her how sorry I am."

"And when you say, 'I just really want . . .,' is that about you or her?" Betsy interjected.

"I guess I'm being selfish and should think about what my mom would want?" I questioned.

"No," Betsy said. "What are your motives for wanting to call your mom—be honest, Kim!"

"Well, I do miss her," I continued. "But if I get really honest . . . I want her to forgive me."

"Yes. Go on," Betsy prompted.

"Fuck! I want her to forgive me, so I can feel better about myself. I know, I know, Betsy, wrong motives!"

To which Betsy reminded me of my hopes, fears, and expectations with my phone call with David, and she stated, "Kim, expectations are nothing more than setups for resentments."

I had to let that one soak in. *So I was never to have expectations?* I wondered.

Explaining to Betsy that I was sure that I'd be okay, regardless of the outcome, I just really wanted to call my mom. She replied, "You're not at that step yet. That's step nine, and what does the second part of step nine say, Kim?"

"I have to say the whole thing out loud? 'We made *direct amends* to such people wherever possible, except when to do so would injure them or others.' So are you saying that if I called her, it may injure her?" I questioned.

"Maybe, Kim, but what else are you missing?" she asked, wanting me to dig deeper.

"Direct amends . . . so like in person? Is that what you mean?"

"Here's what I mean, Kim. Number one, you're not at step nine yet. Remember the steps are in order for a reason. Number two, it says '*where*ver possible' not *when*ever possible. First, we need to explore your expectations which have led to resentments in step four and step five. Then, there are still three more steps to get through before step nine. You're still soaking up how to apply the third step *in all of your affairs.*

"Think of how your expectations set you up for disappointment and heartache in the past. Do you really want to set yourself up for more anger, frustration, and resentment if you don't get the results you'd like from your mom?" she asked.

I didn't reply, but had all kinds of possible scenarios running through my head. As much as I wanted my mom's forgiveness, as much as I longed for reconciliation with her, depending on my mom's response, it could send me over the brink to not just relapse, but to want to kill myself again. I didn't want to feel that way ever again! "You're right, Betsy," I said. This one is going to take TIME. This one is going to have to be a 'thing I must earn.'

Mini Miracles for Everyone!

T uesday, May 5, Betsy treated me to breakfast at the Silver Star before going to the noon meeting over at the YANA Club. It was the first time I had been in there since I walked out after telling my father to fuck off. I was flooded with memories and feelings, and Betsy kept telling me to share them with her as they came up. Her response nearly every time was, "Aren't you happy that you don't have to live like that anymore?" And I was. I liked how she had a way of shifting my perception from thoughts that in the past would have me spiraling into endless negativity, into something positive, something to be grateful for instead.

I also began to notice that I was beginning to do that with others when they'd start to complain or think negatively. I was often able to find *something positive* in the person, place, thing, situation, or experience, and as a result, I felt better.

The parking lot of the club seemed more crowded than usual for a Tuesday. I even said something to Betsy about it as we got out of our cars and walked toward the door. As we walked in, several people yelled "Surprise!" And when I looked to see where it was coming from, there was Chuck and Arlene!

Kitty came out from the side and rounded us up in a huge group hug. Embracing, we spun around in blissful laughter with happy tears coming from all four of us as we spun around and jumped around until we almost fell down from being dizzy.

When we settled, I went to introduce Chuck and Arlene to Betsy when Kitty excitedly exclaimed that Betsy is the one that helped her pull off the surprise and that they even made a cake for Chuck and me whose sobriety dates were a day apart.

That day when the chairperson asked, "Is there anyone celebrating ninety days of continuous sobriety?"

Chuck and I jumped out of our seats, grabbed each other's hands, and with huge grins on our faces, we went up to receive our ninety-day blue poker chips surrounded by Pat from Roy's Palm, Karen, Frank, Old-Timer Rodeo Bill, Kitty, Arlene, and of course, Betsy, and an extended group of drunks and druggies clapping, whistling, and cheering for us. This time when I went up to get a chip, it felt like a celebration of accomplishment filled with hope and promise rather than feeling like a piece of unworthy crap. Chuck and I embraced the chairperson in a group hug, grabbed hands again, and simultaneously held up our blue poker chips while grinning ear to ear. And then from the back of the room, someone yelled, "M&M's for everyone!" And as we all looked to see who it was, Chuck, Arlene, Kitty, and myself let out another gleeful yell as we saw Linda and Jack standing in the back of the room, both of them with bags of M&M's in their hands.

Apparently, Betsy knew them too and arranged for them to come to the celebration if they could make it on their lunch break. Cake, M&M's, and smiles for everyone. This sobriety thing was amazing! Who would have thought?

Wherever Possible

I was in a great mood after celebrating our mini-treatment reunion and Chuck and I receiving our blue poker chips. As Gene and I entered the house that Tracy and I now shared as roommates, the phone rang, and with happiness in my voice, I answered saying, "Hello?"

"Kim? It's your mom." Immediately, I began to shake. My heart felt like it was in my throat, and I immediately plummeted from feelings of elation to extreme guilt.

"Mom?" I questioned back and then immediately started rambling in a shaky voice, "Oh my god, how are you? I am so sorry! Are you okay? Are you out of the hospital? Where are you?"

"I'm okay," she said kind of quietly as I tried to picture the expression on her face.

"You kind of caught me off guard, Mom. I don't even know how to express how sorry I am. It's like there aren't enough words or actions that I think I could say or do that would take away the pain of what I did to you and the suffering you've endured as a result," I said. My mood flipped like a light switch from complete happiness back to guilt and sadness.

"It's going to take some time, Kim. Not so much with me, but definitely for your dad. He's still really angry. I'm just happy that you got help. Tracy told me that today you were celebrating ninety days of continuous sobriety, and I thought today might be a good day to call you, but then, some cops came to the house today looking for you. They have a warrant for your arrest."

"Oh!" I exclaimed.

160

"Apparently, you missed your court date?" she questioned and then went on. "I told them to cancel the warrant. I didn't want to press charges since you had gotten help. And through the grapevine, I knew you were doing well, but they said that's not how it works. I didn't tell them where you were, but you may want to go and turn yourself in."

"Through the grapevine?" I kind of giggled. "Mom, do you remember that weirdo guy Frank that used to come into the restaurant?" I questioned.

"Yes," she kind of giggled too. "What about him?"

"I learned that he did all kinds of things to try and protect us, prayed for us, helped, and fed other people, and that he's actually a really nice, loving, and caring guy."

"Oh, he pulled me aside a couple of times to ask if I was okay—if I needed help with your father's anger. Yes, he is nice. Actually, all the people that came into the Silver Star and regulars out at Roy's Palm have come to see me, check on me and your dad. They made meals and stuff for your dad and brother while I was in the hospital. They're all very nice.

"When I'd ask them about you, Kim, they said they couldn't really say anything, but they did say that you were doing really well. I wanted to call you. I wanted to tell you I had not forgotten, but had forgiven you, and when the cops showed up this morning, it seemed ordained.

"I had the hospital priest saying prayers for you. It was actually the chaplain at the hospital that had people from Al-Anon come to speak with me."

"What?" I questioned.

"Al-Anon is for friends and families of people that have alcohol issues. They came to the hospital, talked with me, gave me literature to read, brought me gifts and flowers, and then I started going to meetings as soon as I was out of the hospital."

"Wow! Really, Mom?" I was excited to learn more.

"I should have taken you kids to Al-Anon a long time ago, but I was afraid to. Too busy to, and in all honesty, I was probably afraid to find out what it was all about. I just never went. The situation that happened between you and me got me into recovery too."

I could hear and feel her smiling through the phone.

"I've been learning all kinds of things about myself, you, and your dad . . . I guess I actually have a lot of amends to make too, but my sponsor said it will take time. Time is an acronym for—"

"Things I must earn," we said at the same time and then started to giggle together.

My fears, my feelings of guilt and the sadness when I first heard my mom's voice on the phone seemed to vanish as my excitement about my mom also being in recovery filled my heart with additional gratitude.

Then, she dropped a bomb. "I hear you're pregnant too. That's exciting. I like David. I'm presuming he's the father?"

"Yes, he is. I called him, but it didn't go well," I responded.

"Well, it's kind of funny how things have a way of working themselves out despite our fears and pains. I mean, look at what's happened as a result of this mess. You are celebrating ninety days of continuous sobriety, your father has gotten serious about recovery again, and I'm in Al-Anon," she said. "I guess God just has to take drastic measures to get our attention sometimes," she added. "Well, I have to go. I just wanted to congratulate you and let you know that I'm really proud of you, that I forgive you and want you and those grandbabies in my life. Oh, I hope you have a girl this time. It's going to be so much fun to go shopping for girly outfits and stuff. I'll be happy with whatever you have though. It will all work out, Kimberly, as long as you stay sober— even with David eventually. It will just take time. T-I-M-E. Time." She giggled. "So when are you going to go turn yourself into the jail?" she asked.

"I suppose I should probably do it as soon as possible, but I want to talk with Tracy about it to make sure Gene will be taken care of in case I have to serve time or something," I responded.

"The cops told me that it's in the state attorney's hands now, and that there was nothing I could do about it. If there was, I would," she said. "Well, call me and let me know, so I can at least come to court and see you, if you'd be okay with that," she asked.

"Oh, if you'd be willing to come up to Sarasota, that would mean a lot to me, Mom!"

And we agreed that I would let her know.

We ended the conversation with telling each other that we loved each other, with intentions of seeing each other in court. After hanging up the phone, I went and swept up Gene who had been playing with his toys near my feet, kissed him all up, and began to cry.

"Why are you crying, Mama?" he asked with a bit of concerned confusion on his face.

"Because I am just so happy that you are my son, and I just love you so much!" I exclaimed.

"I love you too, Mama!" he said, wrapping his arms around me. "You're the best mama ever!" he proclaimed. Hugging, my eyes filled with tears, as the fear of having to serve jail time, away from my little boy, filled me with dread. Gene had already been through enough! I didn't want to be absent from his life ever again—not just physically, but not emotionally either.

Monday, May 11

Tracy and I scrambled to make possible arrangements in case the State had their way with me and decided to lock me up and throw away the key. I went to several meetings a day and was calling Betsy at least twice a day to try and keep my anxiety about my future in check—to stay in the day, to not project my fears. I worked the first three steps in that I was powerless over what would happen. I recognized that I needed to turn this over and believe that I could stay sane through this and turn over the results to the powers that be. I even prayed. I tried to view the whole situation, regardless of whatever the outcome would be, as something that would work out for my highest good. It sure wasn't easy. Like Betsy would say, "Simple, but not always easy."

I found myself writing feverishly to Gene and my unborn baby in my journal. I wanted them to know that regardless of the outcome, that I loved them, they were loveable, and that even if I couldn't be there because I was in jail, that I would eventually get out, and I promised I would never go to jail again. That no matter what, we would eventually be together again. I wrote to them about how things were changing for the better, but that sometimes it takes a tragedy to get our attention when things need to change. I wrote to them expressing that if they were able to recognize these things sooner than I had, that they could see positive results before things had to get *really* bad.

Monday morning, Betsy came and picked me up to take me to the Sarasota County Jail. That prior week, I hugged and kissed Gene as though it may be the last time I was going to see him. I expressed deep and sincere apologies to Tracy for all I had put him through. I expressed deep and sincere appreciation for all the things I appreciated that Tracy and others had done for me over the past one hundred days. And I felt that I was as prepared as I could possibly be to face the consequences that resulted from my substance abuse—my dis-ease, my disease.

In the nicest maternity top I could find and stretchy pants, I walked into the courthouse with my Big Book in my hand and my license and white poker chip in my bra as my security. I walked up to the counter and explained that there was a warrant out for my arrest, that I was turning myself in.

They took my Big Book, my driver's license, and my white poker chip, explaining that I wasn't able to take these things with me, but that they'd get them back to me when and if appropriate. They had me turn around as they put handcuffs on me and led me to a holding cell.

The whole thing seemed surreal, and I found myself feeling calm for some reason, which I still can't explain despite the sound of others in cells, cell doors opening and slamming shut, people yelling obscenities and clanging chains of people that were being put in handcuffs and shackles.

Trying to just breathe while praying and meditating with my eyes closed, I heard the jailer unlocking the door and opened my eyes and then stood up.

"Turn around please," she said as I placed my hands behind my back and put the handcuffs on. "Are these too tight?" she asked.

"No, thank you for asking," I responded, surprised at her kindness as I turned my head over my shoulder to try and see her.

"I'm going to bring you down to the courtroom, where you'll have a seat, and then when your name is called, you walk up to the podium and wait for the judge to speak to you," she instructed as we rode the elevator.

Walking behind me as we made our way into the courtroom, I saw my mom seated in the pew-type benches on the right.

"Mom!" I blurted.

"Hi!" She turned and began to wave, all excited to see me despite the circumstances. I'm sure we both would have preferred a different way to see each other for the first time in months, but she was there for me—standing and looking fantastic despite having suffered a broken hip and jaw. I wanted to go and hug her so bad!

Then, suddenly, I noticed Betsy and Frank were in the seats in front of my mom. Frank did his finger-wave thing, and Betsy put her hands in prayer position up to her lips and gave me a nod and a smile.

"All, rise!" the bailiff's voice boomed, bringing back foggy memories of the last time I appeared in a courtroom. And then I saw him come out from behind what reminded me of the secret wall where the library was hidden at my uncle Arnie and aunt Elsie's home, Judge Two Sugars and a Splash of Cream. I couldn't believe it . . . *my judge.* I thought as I suddenly noticed what appeared to be the same weasel-looking attorney sitting at the table in front of the pews with a stack full of files.

When my name was called, I got up and held eye contact with my mom as I walked to the podium.

The judge said some things about my case. Then, the state attorney began to make their recommendations to pay for the sins of what I had done in my blackout. Then, out of nowhere, my mom stood up and forcefully said, "Your Honor, I do not want to press charges! I was the victim in this case, and I just wanted my daughter to get help, and she has done that. She's been clean and sober now for more than one hundred days . . . and she's pregnant."

Lightly banging his gavel, he nicely asked my mother to take a seat, and the state attorney continued to make their case and recommend charges for me. When he was finished, the judge asked me if I had anything I wanted to say, and I began to cry.

"Your Honor, I know my drunken blackout is no excuse for what I did. However, it was also the catalyst that got me clean and sober. I went to First Step the day that you released me on my own recognizance. Since that time, I have gotten a sponsor.

That's my sponsor up there," I said, pointing to Betsy with my head, since my hands were cuffed behind me. "I go to meetings on a daily basis—actually sometimes more than once a day. I'm working a program of recovery, and my family and I are working on becoming healthier through making this recovery a family thing. I am truly sorry for what happened, but I have to also be honest and tell you that having this happen has been a blessing in disguise, so whatever you deem fit, I will follow. Thank you for the opportunity to speak," I said, making direct eye contact with him this time and smiling.

"I see you're pregnant too?" he smiled and questioned.

"Yes, I am. I'm due October 28."

Then, he looked over at Betsy and asked how she thought I was doing. Betsy kept it short, but she did share how hard I had been working and what great improvements I had made in the time she had been my sponsor.

Then, Two Sugars and a Splash of Cream addressed my mom and wanted to know what she would do if she were in his position, and my mom stood up and said, "Your Honor, I would dismiss this case, and I'll tell you why: I was not the only victim in this case. My daughter was also a victim of repression, abuse, trauma, and her drinking and drugging in my opinion may have originated from that. That being said, like Kim, I also feel like this has been a blessing in disguise, a wake-up call to our whole family. I too have started a recovery program in Al-Anon. My husband, Kim's father, has become more active in recovery again. This event brought our family together, and it would be a shame to see our daughter have to serve time as a result. It seems counterintuitive—counterproductive if you will. That's why I'm here today. I don't want the State to pursue charges, but to drop them so we can get on with our new lives in recovery."

I was blown away by my mother's words and may have even had my mouth hanging open in shock. I don't recall.

"Thank you for asking and allowing me to share," my mom then said and sat down.

Then, the judge asked Weasel-man what he thought, and he went on about battery, disorderly conduct, blah, blah, blah when the judge suddenly interrupted him and said, "Didn't you just hear what her mom said?"

"Yes, Your Honor, but—"

Then, Judge Two Sugars and a Splash of Cream interrupted him again and said some other things, but the thing that I remembered most that came from his mouth was, "I'm dismissing this case." And he banged his gavel, looked up at me, and said, "I wish you and your family the best, Kim, and don't ever let me see you in my courtroom again!"

Smiling, I said, "Thank you, Your Honor!" still in handcuffs. The jailer then led me out of the courtroom as I gave a nod and a smile to my mom, Betsy, and Frank. I didn't know what was going to happen next, and I was in a bit of shock.

When the jailer and I got into the elevator and the door closed, she said, "I have never seen something like that happen, and I've been here a long time. You're really lucky. And I don't normally say anything to people about anything really, but I just want to say, good for you. I also hope everything works out for you and your family. What just happened may never happen again." And the doors opened.

As we got back to a different counter to be released, I turned to her after she took my handcuffs off and said, "Thank you!"

"Best of luck to you," she said, and she walked away through the locked steel door.

A New Day

I walked through the doors into the brilliant sunlight and heard my mom shout, "Kim, I'm over here!"

Betsy and Frank turned to look at me hearing my mom call to me as I appeared out of the courthouse. Betsy blew a kiss, and she and Frank both waved as my mom and I walked toward each other, crying with our arms open and ready to embrace.

We hugged, we cried, we laughed, we pulled away, and then embraced again.

"Let's get something to eat," my mom said as we walked toward her car, both of us replaying the courtroom scene and the unbelievable dismissal by the judge, the look on the state attorney's face when he was shot down, how amazing it was that Betsy was there and how even Frank showed up for support.

Wanting to get back to the house and share with Tracy the results and squeeze my little boy, my mom suggested we go through a drive-through and just grab lunch for all of us and go to the house that Tracy, Gene, and I shared.

Pulling into the driveway, Gene and Angie came running out to greet us with Tracy on their heels. When he saw that I was also getting out of the car, he exclaimed, "Well, this is good!" as I scooped up Gene into my arms and grabbed the bag of food from the front seat.

It was a beautiful, sunny day with low humidity, so we went out to the back porch to eat and share the details of the unbelievable court proceedings. Gene seemed really happy to have us all together, three people that he loved so much and his dog Angie running and playing as though she sensed the happiness and love of this day too.

After we cleaned up and things had settled down a bit, my mom suddenly said, "Oh, I almost forgot. I have something for you, Kimberly," she said, smiling and begun to dig into her huge purse.

I couldn't believe it! I recognized the royal-blue box and thought, *Oh my god! Really? Is it true? Is this really happening?*

With tears in her eyes, she said, "I wanted to give this to you sooner, but was worried that you'd lose it or pawn it, and now just seems like the right time. I love you," she said with tears coming down her cheeks as she handed me the box. "I hope it fits, but if not, we'll get it sized."

There it was. Aunt Elsie's ring, the star bursting forth in the sunlight out of the blue stone, surrounded by eighteen diamonds in a delicate white gold setting. Looking at my mom with Gene and Angie by my side looking to see what was going on, Gene suddenly said, "Wow, Mama, that's sparkly like you!" as I placed it on my finger.

"You think I'm sparkly, Gene?" I asked as I moved my finger around, catching the star in the sunlight.

"Yeah, Mama, I can see the sparklies in your eyes—they're shiny," he smiled and said as he ran off again to play with Angie.

Reaching over to hug my mom, I looked up into the sky and said out loud, "Thank you! Thank you! Thank you!"

What an amazing new life I had been given and the opportunity to have as a result of what I thought had been the worst thing that ever had happened to a person like me.

I didn't care if people thought us recovery people were a cult anymore. I was proud to be a member of the "said cult" that had survived to earn a seat at the table of fellow "cult" members.

I didn't even care when people read or used the *God* word anymore. I had come to an understanding that it was okay for us to have a god of our own understanding and that could pretty much be anything if it kept us from picking up a drink, a drug, or kept us from some other obsessive-compulsive behavior.

I didn't mind doing the steps Betsy's way. Don't get me wrong. They certainly weren't easy. Not only were they keeping me sober, but they had changed the way I had perceived my life and the world. The steps Betsy had me do gave me insight and awareness into myself and even into others. These steps were teaching me empathy for my fellow earth dwellers and teaching me not to take things so personally.

I didn't mind the meetings like I thought I would in the beginning and thought it would be impossible to go for ninety days in a row and then actually ended up going to more than one hundred in those first ninety days. The meetings were where I actually discovered I could make and had made new friends that were learning new ways to live that the normies and a lot of other people didn't seem as fortunate to have.

I didn't mind the hugging anymore either. In fact, I had become a hugger myself—like Frank.

I also found myself laughing more, feeling genuinely happy, despite the things I had done in my past. I was experiencing M&M's, and I think even though I wasn't yet at step nine, some of those "promises" seemed to be coming true.

I had allowed GOD, a "group of drunks and druggies," to love me enough to a point where I was actually beginning to love myself—not in an external vain way, but in a way that came from the inside out and not the outside in. I was discovering that I was in fact smart, caring, kind, compassionate, empathetic, and even insightful. And to make matters even better, my son thought I was sparkly. Like Linda had reminded me, I needed to stay in the light in order to shine.

It had taken me a lifetime of blaming people, places, things, situations, and waking up in a jail cell out of a blackout to get my attention. I'm grateful that no one died in the process, and even though it hadn't been but over one hundred days, I was on my way. I was being given this gift of finding a new way to live, a life of being truly happy, of changing the patterns of drunken violence that had kept generations of my family stuck in dysfunction.

I was giving my children the opportunity to grow up with love, hope, peace, and the possibility for a much better life than I had.

I didn't want this sobriety thing. I didn't think I needed treatment. I wasn't going to go to meetings, get a sponsor, work those steps, but what I discovered was Karen was right, the night I picked up my white chip when she said, "You're going to love this way of life, Kim." And she was right.

Epilogue

Addiction can manifest itself in a variety of ways. Sometimes addiction has nothing to do with a substance or substances, but manifests itself in other compulsions, obsessions and ways of thinking, feeling and behaving. The common theme is how these compulsions or obsessions in thoughts, feelings and behaviors negatively impact our lives and the lives of those around us.

Since the founding of Alcoholics Anonymous in 1935, more than 248 different twelve step groups have sprung up around the globe. Many use a slight variation of Alcoholics Anonymous' original twelve steps as their primary guidelines for creating positive change in an individual's life.

Expressed in the previous pages are the possibilities and potentialities of 'practicing these principles (of the twelve steps) in all of our affairs', not only as it relates to substances, but 'in *all* of our affairs'.

In the promises (quoted in the previous pages from Alcoholics Anonymous), it says that the promises will '*always* materialize *if* we work for them.' The small two letter word 'if' in this instance, carries a lot of personal responsibility in that we must do the work.

There are no magic pills. There are no magic spells. There are no magic wands. Work is necessary to evoke personal insight, growth and change.

I hope that in sharing this part of my journey with you, that you are inspired to learn more about how you can use the twelve step's principles, concepts and philosophies to live the life you deserve to live.

It is also my hope that those working with addicts and particularly those within the judicial system, will consider looking at the *whole* individual rather than just the behaviors that get us incarcerated in the first place. I hope that in sharing my story, more addicts and their families can be helped by erasing the stigmatization that often comes with being an addict.

Like my original sponsor, Betsy, shared with me from the start, "Recovery is simple, but not necessarily easy." However, I am a living testimony that given the opportunity, positive change is possible and it can be for you also!

Thank you for reading my story and may you experience bowls full of M&M's on your journey!

Shine on with light and love,
Kim del Valle Walker

To contact Kim, please e-mail her at kimdvwalker@gmail.com
Or find her on Facebook @kimdvwalker
Thank you!

Websites for Additional Information

Alcoholics Anonymous: www.aa.org
Al-Anon: www.alanon-maryland.org
Narcotics Anonymous: www.na.org
Nar-Anon: www.nar-anon.org
Co-dependents Anonymous: www.coda.org
Adult Children of Alcoholics: www.adultchildren.org

About the Author

D rug addict and now person in long-term recovery, Kim Walker's bottom was the catalyst that motivated her to go back to college, become a licensed addiction counselor, holistic health practitioner, speaker and published author. With now over thirty years of experience teaching, providing workshops and assisting individuals, couples and families in addiction and spiritual matters. Kim believes that instead of asking "what's wrong with you?" we should be asking, "what happened to you?" and "what's right with you?" She believes that with HELP (Helping to Empower the Lives of People), we can transform many of the issues we face that result from trauma and addiction.

CPSIA information can be obtained
at www.ICGtesting.com
Printed in the USA
LVHW030901040319
609387LV00003B/308/P

9 781642 148718